COACHING KIDS' HOCKEY

John,
 I've really enjoyed having you, Tricia & Jake on so many great hockey teams. Here's a story I'm sure you can relate to. Hope you enjoy it.
 All the best,
 Peter

COACHING KIDS' HOCKEY

THE GOOD, THE BAD, AND THE UNBELIEVABLE

BY
T.J. O'GRADY

KOOKABURRA
PRESS

© 2005 by T.J. O'Grady

All rights reserved. The use of any part of this publication reproduced, transmitted in any form or by any means, electronic, mechanical, photocopying, recording, or otherwise, or stored in a retrieval system, without the prior written consent of the publisher—or, in the case of photocopying or other reprographic copying, a licence from the Canadian Copyright Licensing Agency—is an infringement of the copyright law.

National Library of Canada Cataloguing in Publication Data
O'Grady, T. J., 1958-
Coaching Kids Hockey: The Good, The Bad and the Unbelievable
/ T.J. O'Grady.
ISBN 0-9736455-0-4
1. Hockey for Children-Coaching. 2. Hockey Coaches.
I. Title.
GV848.5.O37A3 2004   796.962'07'7   C2004-906039-2

Printed in Canada.

Published by Kookaburra Press
Suite 1406, 1011 Upper Middle Road East,
Oakville, Ontario Canada

Visit www.coachingkidshockey.com.

For Sarah, Joe and Mike

ACKNOWLEDGEMENTS

Only in trying to get a book published do you realize writing is anything but a solitary experience.

It all started with Karen Jackson, who upon hearing I was attempting to write a book, instantly gave me two pieces of advice—take a course in creative writing and join a writers' group. She recommended the course, and then brought me into her own writers' group. For the year it took to create the manuscript, Karen continued to provide intelligent guidance and fittingly came up with the idea for the book's title. Thank you Karen.

I'm also deeply indebted to the other members of our group—Jane Petrovich, Will Leskowich, Marie Macneill and Mark Offer—who despite being anything but hockey fans, enthusiastically reviewed the story every two weeks and made so many improvements to the original manuscript.

I suspect other writers will agree that when a designer creates a cover, you begin to believe the book will see the light of day. Special thanks go to Laura Brady not just for the book design and typesetting, but also for so many practical pieces of advice relating to the business end of publishing.

I'd also like to thank my editor, Mark Clayton, a hockey fan, player and parent, who made countless suggestions to improve the manuscript.

Any time you step outside your normal range of activities, the reactions of those closest to you determines how far you'll go. My family has been amazingly supportive throughout, especially my mother who helped get the practical aspect of publishing under way at a time when she was under great personal distress.

My wife Liz has patiently watched and waited as next week turned into next month turned into next year. This was never her project but she supported it unwaveringly, never once suggesting I abandon it for more practical uses of my time. I am indeed lucky and very grateful.

Finally, a hockey season is a panoply of events, some of which showcase humans at their finest, some of which don't. The kids and adults who lived this story are all decent people I enjoyed spending the year with. Once I decided it was a story that ought to be told, I felt I had to remain truthful to all events in order to give the reader an accurate portrayal. I thank the players, parents and others for recognizing that certain of their actions were included not so much to comment on them as individuals but rather, to present the situation in its fullness.

COACHING KIDS' HOCKEY

KEEP YOUR STICK ON THE ICE

I'm not a big believer in hockey as a metaphor for life, but I must admit, when you keep your stick on the ice, you never know what will happen. Whether it's hockey or anything else.

In January 2001, it occurred to me that I should coach a minor hockey team. My seven-year-old son Michael was playing Tyke in our town's House League with 127 other kids. The hockey was the sort that's entertaining only to parents of the boys on the ice. Passes were rare, shots weak and the flow virtually non-existent.

Like most hockey dads, I played in my youth and still follow the pros. When my first son, Joe, turned three, I introduced him to the game in our basement. Sure enough, he loved it. We graduated to road hockey, then onto the ice by age six. Mike, two years younger, followed in his brother's footsteps and, if anything, even more keenly. Soon I was taking them to ponds, public skating and, last year, our first backyard rink. Coaching seemed like a natural progression.

At the time I'd already coached soccer for years—over two

hundred boys and girls aged five to fourteen. I'd even acquired a reputation among the parents, not just for winning, but also for teaching their son or daughter the game—including both fundamentals and team play. The funny thing is I'd never played soccer. I had to learn it from the ground up in order to teach the kids. Books, videos, Web sites—I used whatever educational material I could find. I volunteered only because my daughter's teams never passed, and it frustrated me to watch them. That was a game I didn't know.

Hockey, on the other hand, is my favourite game. There's a flow to it that makes it fun to watch and fun to play. But that January, after four months of watching Mike and his teammates, I could see none of them were getting any closer to finding that flow. I wasn't noticing any big improvement in individual skills either. I'd never thought about volunteering before, mainly because hockey parents are often a handful. But this year I was getting to know many of them. It no longer seemed intimidating.

"Hey Mike," I said one Saturday night, "what would you think if I was your hockey coach?"

"It'd be great," he replied, without hesitation. "Can you?"

"Maybe. Your league is going to need coaches next year."

That was the crux of the matter. Getting accepted was usually pretty difficult. Whereas soccer coaches are in short supply—few adults in Canada know anything about the game—hockey is entirely different. It's our national sport. Most Canadians feel they know everything about hockey and want to share it with their kids. More people apply to coach than are needed.

But circumstances had conspired to create a shortage in Mike's age group. At the end of the season, thirty-four boys would be chosen to leave the House League and form two Rep teams, to play against squads from other towns. Four coaches had sons certain to be picked, so the House League would need four new coaches.

I asked around to find out how to get my name in, and what I could do to improve the odds of being accepted.

"They like you to be certified," said a parent on Joe's team, referring to a coaching licence. "It's not hard but you have to give up a weekend."

"It helps to know somebody," offered another.

I didn't know anyone who worked for the league and normally shy away from anything that requires me to give up family time. But I was on sabbatical; all my time was family time. If ever I could afford to give up a weekend, it was now. And the reason I took a year off was to do things I'd never had time for—like coach hockey. All in all it had the feel of something that was meant to be.

Then came the unexpected.

"Are you going to let Michael play Rep?" asked another parent as we sat in the stands.

Rep hockey. What little I knew didn't sound too appealing. The practices were tough, with lots of skating and coaches who scream at kids. The games could be two hours away. The cost would be triple what I was paying for House League.

"No. I don't think so," I replied.

It was more than logistics. The way I look at kids' hockey reflects my own experience. Hockey's a great game that becomes too violent for decent people once they hit their teens. I'd been completely open and honest with both Mike and Joe. I started playing when I was seven. I was better than average, won a few championships and a couple of scoring titles, but quit when I was thirteen because there were fights in literally every period of every game. Frankly, I was having more fun playing road hockey.

So truthfully, there didn't seem to be any reason for Mike to play Rep. In all probability he would quit hockey in a few years. Spending the extra time and money seemed pointless. Hockey was just a game he was playing at this stage of his life—for fun.

Unfortunately, my son has two attributes that allow him to excel despite his father. First, he has a mind for games. He even likes chess. Mike listens to the rules, experiments and then arrives at a strategy. In hockey, it means no one has to tell him to pass. He wants to win, and passing is a pretty obvious way to win.

Second, when it comes to speed, he was born lucky. Unlike me, Mike has the muscles that make him naturally fast. He's not an elegant skater, but he makes up for it with leg strength and coordination.

By January, he'd caught up to the kids who'd played summer hockey, or were on the ice five times a week to his two. He'd figured out how to use his teammates and his speed to score goals. His coach put him at centre. People noticed. When his team pulled their goalie, Mike skated out as the extra attacker. Over the second half of the season, he was Top Ten in league scoring.

Then people heard about the dad who wasn't pushing his son hard enough.

"You've *got* to let that kid play Rep," declared a parent, after seeing Mike score twice in one game. "He's got more upside than anyone." The parent was a dad who coached an older boy's Rep team, someone who knew what he was talking about. "All these other kids are getting extra ice time, extra coaching. Mike isn't. Imagine what he'll be like when he does. You've got to do it."

My conviction wavered. Watching Mike succeed conjured up memories of my own youth. I played numerous sports and won trophies in virtually every one. But I never pursued any in depth. I've often wondered what might have happened if I did. What if my parents had pushed me? I began to wonder if I should be pushing Mike.

"There's nothing wrong with letting him try out," said my wife. "He can see whether it's something he likes. Then if they offer him a spot, he can say yes or no."

I agreed.

The Rep tryouts didn't begin until four weeks after the season ended. What went on in those four weeks was farcical. Virtually all of the Rep-parent wannabes enrolled their sons in intensive hockey instruction, anywhere from one to four weeks at a cost of two to three hundred dollars per week. The tryouts are essentially six practices before the skates are put away for the summer. So these parents were spending up to one thousand dollars to get their son in peak condition for six practices. I didn't want to sabotage Mike's chances but there was no way I was doing that. Instead, I splurged on two nights of public skating at a cost of two dollars per night, but I did lead Mike through some stops and starts.

The first tryout was just as strange—sixty kids on the ice run through a myriad of skating drills. But the only competitive aspects were a few races near the end. Since Mike won all of his, I had little doubt he'd be invited back for the second tryout. I was wrong.

"He needs to work on his skating," the coach told Mike and me. Nothing more. I was stunned. How can you tell a player who won all his races to work on his skating? But Mike wasn't fazed at all. He bounced out of the arena and talked about other things on the ride home.

Two hours later, I received a call from the coach of the second team. He wanted to make sure Mike would still try out for his team. I didn't want another rejection so I asked him point blank—would Mike make the team? His response was immediate. Unlike the other coach, he had been to every game and knew the boys, including how good my son was. Mike would have no trouble making the team.

A week later we found ourselves back at the rink for another tryout. This one involved scrimmages, where Mike shows best. After two times on the rink, the coach stopped me outside the dressing room and said in a clear voice: "I'd like your son on the team. I'm not going to card him right now, but don't worry, he's made the team."

Now that was more like it. I hadn't been convinced Rep hockey was the way to go, but I must admit, I was proud of Mike for making the team. On the drive home I told him so. We even stopped for an ice cream cone to celebrate. Over the next few months Mike told family and friends he'd be playing Rep hockey this coming year. The way he said it, I got the sense he was proud of himself too. All notions of me coaching hockey vanished.

In August, I heard most of the Rep kids were enrolled in at least two different hockey schools, something I'd never done. I put Mike and Joe in a one-week skating camp—an hour a day of skating without pucks. It was there I ran into the manager of the Rep team, a fellow I've known for years.

"I tell you T.J.," he said, "it's the weirdest thing. I keep running into people who didn't get carded but think they've made the team."

A hollow feeling formed in the pit of my stomach. "Well, Mike's not carded," I replied, "but the coach definitely said he made the team."

The man's colour suddenly changed. I could see he felt awkward. Then he told me he'd spoken to the coach just two days ago and he was certain. The only players who made the team were the ones already carded. "Everyone else has to try out again. It's next week. He has five spots left."

It would have been easy to pick up the phone, call the coach and remind him of our conversation. I thought about it. I even looked up his number in the phone book. But I didn't. Mike would be with this man for six months. A kid's coach is one of his influences. I wanted to know exactly what this man's character was. I knew what he said and the words he used. It was a very memorable conversation. Either he was a man of honour or not, I wasn't going to force him to keep his word. And there's no way I wanted Mike playing for a coach who didn't want him.

The tryouts, again mostly scrimmages, went well. On the

second day, Mike not only outscored everyone but took the puck off several players who'd already been carded. No less than three other parents came up to me and shook my hand, saying it was obvious Mike made the team. I was proud of him. No camps, no summer leagues and still, top scorer in the tryouts.

"How do you think you played?" I asked him on the way home.

Mike shrugged. "Okay I guess."

"Okay?" I laughed. "Mike, if they don't take you now, they're either blind or stupid."

That night, the phone rang. It was the team manager. He wanted to give me a heads-up. Unless Mike played better tomorrow, he wouldn't make the team. I didn't know whether to laugh or cry. "Thanks for telling me," I answered calmly.

I really should have expected as much. Our town has a reputation for making weird player selections. We didn't want Mike to go to the final tryout, hoping to shield him from the rejection, but he was adamant. He hoped his play would convince the coaches they were making a mistake. It didn't.

"Nobody passed me the puck," he claimed afterward. It was true. He played left wing and, for the most part, stayed on his side. But in tryouts, no one passes. In fact, many fathers tell their sons not to. Mike rarely touched the puck and the third scrimmage was his worst of the three.

As Mike and I walked into the dressing room for the official verdict, two of the three coaches immediately turned away. From their expressions it was clear they were expecting a scene. So all three men knew the situation. An eight-year-old boy had been told he'd made the team. Now they were going to cut him. A good lesson on adults keeping their word.

"I'd like to AP him," said the head coach, looking me straight in the eye. That's rep-speak for he didn't make the team but he can come to our practices. I hated letting him off easy but there was nothing in it for me, or for Mike, to cause trouble. So I just nodded and told him no thanks. Coming to another team's practices, seeing them in their rep jackets and jerseys, hearing about their games and constantly being reminded you didn't make it, wasn't exactly tempting. I later found out that of the six families offered this "opportunity," we were the only one to turn it down.

Mike said almost nothing on the ride home. When I asked him point blank, he claimed it didn't bother him that much. Then as we crossed the front porch into our house, he turned and said: "So you'll be my coach then?"

My heart sank. It was late August. They ask the House League coaches to apply in May. With the season starting in a few weeks, it was inconceivable the coaches hadn't been chosen.

"We'll see," I replied.

I called the league office first thing the next morning. The conversation lasted less than a minute. The coaches had been picked weeks ago. However, one of them had asked for an assistant. His name was Sean, and they suggested I introduce myself at the coaches' kick-off meeting in a week. They'd be happy to put Mike and I on his team. It wasn't ideal but at least I'd be on the bench.

The kick-off meeting was a perfunctory affair where the league officials tell everyone to behave themselves, think of the kids, follow the rules, etc. A friend pointed Sean out to me soon after I arrived. We chatted briefly and sat together for the meeting. He'd asked for help since he was worried that coaching would interfere with his job.

The only surprise occurred after we broke off with the other coaches for our age group. We met Rose, the convenor assigned to our division to monitor play and ensure everything runs according to the rules. After introducing herself, Rose said she'd already drawn up the teams. She felt she'd been fair to everybody by allocating the names on a purely random basis.

"You definitely don't want to do that," replied one of the returning coaches.

"Definitely not," echoed another.

Much debate ensued, primarily between three men who coached last year. In the end, it was decided to scrap Rose's teams and use a new approach. On the first weekend of play, they'd ask every boy to perform a series of skating and shooting drills. A consistent group of coaches would rate every boy on each drill and these ratings would be used to compile the teams.

As an assistant, I didn't feel it was my place to protest but I could see this wasn't a great plan. The fastest boy through pylons isn't necessarily the fastest boy in a game. When it was clear none of the head coaches were going to protest, I finally expressed my concern. All approaches had flaws, I was told by the voices of authority. This was the best way to go.

So at ten o'clock the following Saturday morning, Mike and I arrived at one of the older arenas in town for an hour of drills. By coincidence, Sean was there too. I joined him by the glass, but he seemed nervous. His son Patrick had already been over to see him twice complaining about cold feet.

"It is the coldest rink in town," I offered, trying to be polite. The arena gets pretty frosty in January, but on this day it was hot outside. I actually enjoyed the cool air.

"I don't know if he's going to make Gold," said Sean, soberly. Our town splits its House League in two. The top half, based on player ratings, goes into Gold and the balance to Silver. Patrick had played Silver the previous year. Thinking his son was ready to move up, Sean had applied to coach a Gold team.

I watched Patrick skate. He wasn't the best but he looked good enough to be in the top half. "I don't think you have anything to worry about," I said, honestly.

But sure enough, a couple of minutes later, Patrick was back. This time he complained his skates were too tight. "New skates," said Sean. "I knew I should've waited."

I watched Sean untie, then retie, Patrick's skates. No other kid had come off once, let alone three times. The session was barely ten minutes old. I must admit that if it had been my son, I'd be embarrassed.

The drills were rudimentary and Mike was bored stiff. The kids spent most of their time standing in line. Patrick managed to stay with the rest of the boys for the balance of the session but repeatedly glanced at, or skated by, his father. Each time he was met with a nod or a finger point, to indicate where his attention should be directed. By the end of the session, Sean was convinced Patrick wouldn't be rated high enough to play Gold.

Mike couldn't wait to get out of the rink, and we hurried home for lunch. An hour later, the phone rang. It was Sean.

"Hey T.J. You know what—I think I'm going to give it a pass this year."

"Give what a pass?"

"The coaching. You know it's such crap with all the politics you have to go through. It's just not worth it you know? And I'm so busy at work I won't have the time. Not this year."

Sean couldn't have seen any politics yet. Not at this stage. And surely he knew the time commitment before signing up. Was he worried about Patrick? Maybe. But I didn't get the feeling he wanted to talk about it.

"Anyway," continued Sean, "they're meeting at the league offices to draft the teams. I can't make it. Is there any chance you can go?"

"I guess, but . . ." I was about to say I'm not a coach.

"Great. And can you let Rose know I won't be coaching? I tried to get hold of her but there's no answer."

"Sean, I can't tell her you quit."

"Yeah, I know. But she isn't picking up. Can you at least warn her she needs to find someone else?"

I agreed, at the same time wondering if there was any way I could slot into the coaching position Sean was giving up. There didn't seem to be anything in particular to do—just keep my stick on the ice and head for the net.

I arrived at the league's office at one thirty, feeling somewhat like a party crasher. The front door was open but there was no one in the reception area. I wandered into a large conference room at the back, but it too was empty. There were no posters, banners, pennants or sweaters. It reminded me of a meeting room in a mid-sized company—one that still had to watch its pennies—more than a hockey office. Had I not passed a couple of trophies on the way in, I'd be wondering if I was in the right place.

At 1:35 P.M., Rose arrived. She's close to retirement age and has a kind face. She smiles when she speaks, whether she's saying something you'll want to hear or not. I gave her Sean's news.

"I'm not surprised," she said. "He told me he might have to back out. But you understand, I have to hear it from him before it's official."

"He said he tried to call you."

"He can try again. Until he tells me in person, he'll be the coach on record. But didn't you say you were interested in coaching?"

My heart beat a little faster. "That's right," I replied. "I've done a lot of coaching before. It's fun. I like it."

Rose stared directly at me, as if trying to ascertain whether I had what it takes to coach a boys' hockey team. "Well," she started, "if Sean does want to give up this team, and he decides to actually tell me himself, then I suppose I'll need another coach." Once again she paused and looked directly into my eyes. It felt odd being given the once over, but at the same time, there was a calmness about her that made me think it was her way of trying to look out for the kids. "You can be the coach of this team if you like."

"Great," I replied without hesitation, feeling like I should say something more. But all I could think was: this is the first hockey thing that has gone right in a long time. She'd offered me the job, I said yes. Score.

"So we'll put your Michael on the team and of course you'll have to take Sean's boy, Patrick. Your team number is five. You'd better write that down."

So that was it. On September 22, 2001, I became a minor hockey league coach. Listening as names were slotted into each team, it occurred to me I'd be in exactly the same spot had I decided not to let Mike try out for Rep. With one major difference. My son, the boy I'm supposed to look out for, wouldn't have suffered the shot to his ego. While I was happy to finally get a team, it bugged me that I'd allowed myself to be sucked into the whole Rep hockey experience. In the end, Mike paid the price.

My goal, with every team I've coached, is to make it a good season for the kids. But my first year as a hockey coach had to be even better. I had to make it up to Mike. I had to prove that I could do this, and not just to myself. Anytime a new coach comes out of the woodwork, everyone knows why. Because he thinks he can do better. Which was true, I did. Now I had to prove it.

ROOKIE COACHING

"Hey Mike," I yell as I arrive home from the meeting. "Guess who your new coach is."

He runs into our front hall, smiling. "You?" he asks.

"That's right. It's not for sure, for sure," I say, remembering Sean has to officially resign. "But I'm pretty sure."

"Alright," he says, wrapping his skinny arms around my waist. "So who's on our team?"

"Here, have a look," I say, handing him the player list.

As Mike scans the list I head for the phone. One of the last surprises at the coaches' meeting had been the timing of my first practice. It's less than eighteen hours away at quarter after eight tomorrow morning. So the first order of business is to let the parents know. I grab a piece of paper to list the things I need to tell them.

"Hey, Will's on our team," says Mike, pleased that a school chum has made the list. "And Connor, Travis . . ."

"Travis is supposed to be good at hockey," I reply, knowing what Mike's first thought will be. Travis was on our soccer team and struggled.

"Joel too!"

"Yeah, I'll probably get his dad to help."

"Wow, I already know five guys on my team. I can't believe it."

Mike returns the player list and I start dialing, glancing at the short note I've made: *Practice tomorrow, 8:15 A.M., Main Arena, Team 5.*

The calls go well. The parents I speak to are friendly and glad to be part of the team. Halfway through, talking with Tommy's dad, I get my first assistant coach. Both Mike and Joe know Tommy, our goalie. They tell me he's good. My wife says the family goes to our church and I'll recognize the dad.

"I don't like to force myself on you or anything," he says, "but I've coached at least five different teams, have my trainer's licence and have been playing for about twenty-five years now, including fifteen as a goalie. If you need any help, let me know."

I may be a rookie but even I can spot a no-brainer. "Great," I reply. "How about tomorrow?"

His name's Brad and, all in all, sounds like a great guy. I give him a quick rundown of the rest of the team, the other coaches and how the draft went.

When I get to Sean, he volunteers to be the other assistant, but I'm reluctant. All I know about him is that he signed up to coach a hockey team, and then backed out at the last minute. Still, I ask him to help with our first few practices. The person I'd intended to pick is proving controversial.

When Joel landed on our team, my first thought was to ask his dad George to be an assistant. We've known each other for years. I coached his older son in soccer and we won a few championships together. I enjoy his sense of humour and, when it comes to sports, we think alike. However, at the end of the draft, a couple of coaches told me not to use him. They said George is too loud for this age group and neither parents nor kids will appreciate it. When I got home, my neighbour, who also knows

George, agreed with the coaches. "His heart's in the right place," he added, "but he just has too much of an edge."

George is a big man and when he has something to say at a sporting event, he bellows it across the field or arena, loud enough that all spectators hear. It's never bothered me because frankly, he's usually right, and most of the time he does it in a way that makes everyone laugh. But now I'm spooked. I ask my wife what she thinks. She knows exactly what the others are referring to and says it's a tough call. If I do ask him, she suggests I have a talk with him first.

Talk with an adult, telling him how to behave. I try to picture how that would go. "Uh, George, some people think you're too aggressive with kids." I laugh when I think of his likely response. "What? Just 'cause I like to cuff the little pissers upside the head every now and then?"

When I call George, his response is exactly as expected. "Beauty. So does this mean we're coaching together?"

"You'd want to coach Joel?" I reply, feebly. "I thought you'd be helping out with Doug's team." Doug is his older son whom he coached last year.

"No. They won't let me. Same old crap. This town's so political. I got teams begging me to coach—Rep teams. But do you think these guys'll give me a chance? No way. Drives me crazy. Every year I put in my application, they don't even call."

George has friends and family in the town next to ours. That's where he coached last year. They finished first and won the championship. I didn't know he'd been applying to coach in our town.

"Let me make sure I've got the team," I reply, explaining the situation. "It should be any day. Sean promised he'd call today or tomorrow. I can't do anything till then."

"Okay. Sure. No pressure, eh?"

I can tell he knows I'm stalling. It probably bugs him. But with everyone telling me to pick someone else, it's suddenly a tough decision. And the truth is, I don't have this team. Not officially. I decide to put off the George decision until Sean resigns.

The rest of the calls are uneventful except that no less than three parents are surprised their kids were in Gold. The first two are happy but the third is a little less than ecstatic.

"No that's not right," he says. "The boy can't skate."

"They saw him this morning," I reply. "They put him in Gold."

"No. Sorry. You've got the wrong Braeden."

I don't recall seeing another Braeden, but just to be sure I skim over the master list. "Nope. He's the only one. It's him."

"Are you sure you're coaching a Gold team?"

"Yes, I'm sure."

"On the piece of paper," continues the dad, "can you actually see the word Gold?"

I glance at the player list and sure enough the word "Gold" is nowhere to be found. For the briefest of moments, I actually wonder. But no. "Look, your son made Gold," I insist. "If you don't think he's up to it, we can move him. But you should at least let him try."

"Okay," concedes the dad before hanging up, "but you'll see what I mean."

After our Rep experience, it's refreshing to speak to parents who aren't trying to push their sons as hard as they can, and see them for what they truly are. But later, it occurs to me that if the parents are surprised their sons made Gold, I might be too. And that may not be a good thing.

In any event, I need to buy a few things for practice. The league dictates that every adult on the ice must wear a helmet. I stopped playing long ago, but last year a second hand store gave me a helmet for free. With a crack in the side, they couldn't sell it. The price was right but the colour wasn't—bright red. It made for quite a sight, especially with my red hair and wire-rimmed glasses. There's no way I'm going in front of parents wearing that. Instead, I'll splurge on a new, preferably cheap, *black* helmet, along with pucks and pylons.

It's my daughter Sarah's birthday so once I'm done the shopping; the five of us head out for a family dinner at a local eatery. By eight thirty we're back home. I still haven't figured out what I'll be doing with a team full of eight-year-olds tomorrow morning, so I grab a few sheets of paper and head for my favourite easy chair, in front of the TV.

I quickly recall drills I've seen other coaches do, but I want this year to be different and I don't want to be the kind of coach who just does what everyone else does.

Objectives I write on the first page, betraying my business background. My hand scribbles whatever comes to mind. *Have fun, be part of a team, win, score goals.* Then comes *a hard wrist shot, pass accurately, get the puck in front of the net, skate backwards.* Looking it over, I can see the objectives fall into two categories—individual and team. I reach for another sheet of paper.

This time I write *Individual Skills* at the top. It strikes me that the easiest way to break them down is to create three baskets. I jot down *Skating, Shooting and Stickhandling.* Immediately I think of checking. This is a non-contact league but still, there should be stick checking. Under stickhandling I write *one-on-ones, keep away* and *stick checking.* Both Mike and Joe love to play keep away and both are great stickhandlers.

Under skating I write: *forward, backward, stop (both sides), crossovers, quick turns, quick starts.* Under shooting: *forehand pass, backhand pass, wrist shot, flip shot, backhand high, three holes in every player.* Then I go back to stickhandling and add: *heads up, sweep move, deke, stop with puck, quick turn with puck.*

Looking over the list, it doesn't seem like much—not for a whole season. But it's all I can think of. Still, separating the skills into three groups seems like a good idea. It keeps things simple.

What if we run our practices that way? I've never seen it done but why couldn't we split the ice into three stations: one for skating, one for stickhandling and one for shooting? I'll put a coach at each station. The players spend ten minutes at one, and then move to the next—thirty minutes in total. That'll leave twenty minutes to work on team skills.

The more I picture it in my mind, the more I like it. With fifteen skaters on the team there'll be five at each station—perfect. Small groups mean less waiting and less trouble. One parent to five kids means the kids have a better chance of learning. Also, they'll get more time to practice the skill. And the dads will be teaching the same thing over and over so they'll get better at teaching. The goalie can stay at the shooting station where he'll get more shots than he would at most practices. Now I'm getting excited.

I reach for another sheet of paper. Across the top I write *Team Skills*. The first thing that comes to mind is something I've used in soccer: *small-sided games*. I've never seen it done in hockey but I don't know why. Some coaches claim that with only half the ice to practice on, there isn't enough room. I'm not so sure. It doesn't need to take up a lot of space. Besides, what choice is there? Team skills are no different than individual skills. They have to be taught in small pieces. Start the player off in a one-on-one. He'll see how tough it is. Add a teammate to make it two-on-one. Immediately he'll see that using a partner makes it much easier to score. It's worked for me over and over. I don't care if other hockey coaches won't do it, or if my parents haven't seen it. I'm definitely trying it. I jot down *one-on-ones, two-on-ones, three-on-twos, etc.*

The next team skill that comes to mind is an obvious one. *Get the puck out of your own end.* Then I add *fast*. Thinking further, I tack on *up the boards*. It makes me think of Mike's team last year. They just couldn't do this. Many of Joe's teams struggled with it too. Visions of players carrying the puck in front of their own net appear in my mind. I promise myself if I do one thing this year, it's make sure every kid on this team knows how to clear the puck out of their own end.

Get the puck in front of the other team's net is another obvious team skill. But what else do I include? How much could a team of eight-year-olds handle? I write down *breakout* but I'm not sure. A set play to get the puck out of your own end is probably too much. It's just an extension of shooting the puck up the boards, so in theory it's doable. But on Joe's team last year, he was the only winger who ever went to the boards consistently in his own end. And they were a year older. There's no harm in trying, but we'll see how good they get at shooting the puck up the boards first. I write down *using defence on the attack*, but it's scarcely on the page before I shake my head. Getting eight-year-olds to pass backwards? Not a chance.

I'm sure I've missed things, but it's more than enough to get us going. I pick two simple drills for each of tomorrow's stations, drawing them out on a separate piece of paper to give to Brad and Sean in the morning. For the team skills, we'll do three-on-twos—a drill that resembles a game situation with three players acting like forwards and two like defencemen. It's also an easy way to introduce forwards to the concept of getting the puck in front of the net, and the defencemen to shooting the puck up the boards. Once done, I glance at the TV. It's past ten o'clock. The news is on. As I sink back in the chair, I'm still thinking about the team. What does Mike really want? What do they all want? I grab another sheet of paper.

Perfect season, I write in the middle. I draw a bunch of spokes around it. *Equal ice time,* I write at the end of one spoke. *Get to play centre,* on another. The ideas come more quickly: *get to start a game, get to end a game, play different positions, power play, penalty kill, warm up goalie.*

Suddenly I see the pattern. Treat every player the same and make sure each one experiences the different aspects of the game. Rotate positions, rotate who gets to start, give everyone a chance to warm up the goalie. The kids will love it.

What about centre? It is a tough position—you have to help out on defence and anchor the offence. Coaches routinely put the best players there, and usually wouldn't dream of allowing their worst players to try it, even for a shift. But nothing bugs me more than an eleven-year-old who's been stuck in one position his whole life. Standing at centre ice and taking a faceoff is a unique part of hockey. These are eight-year-olds. If I can't give every kid a turn at centre, something's wrong. In fact, I'm going to give every kid an entire game at centre. Sixteen kids make up the team, including the goalie. With three lines, it will take six weeks to give each player their game at centre. I'll need that long to figure out what position they're best at anyway. We'll do it.

It's now past eleven and I call it a night. I put my skates, new black helmet, pucks and pylons in the van. I leave Mike's equipment bag in the front hall where I know I'll trip over it, if I don't see it. I'm not exactly a morning person.

Once in bed, sleep is hard to come by. I'm excited. I can't wait to see how this station idea pans out. And what the kids look like. My mind runs through the practice over and over again. Then I move on to future practices, different ideas, other drills to run. It's one thirty when I check the clock for the last time. But I'm out of bed well before the alarm rings.

The Main Arena is the oldest in the city. With its thick wooden rafters and fold-up seats—it feels like an old-time hockey rink. The stands circle the entire ice surface giving the impression good teams play here—teams that people pay to see. Nonetheless, one feature has made the rink famous amongst players and coaches alike—the step down onto the ice surface. It doesn't matter where you step onto the ice—it's still a good twelve inches down. I've never fallen, but it's something I'm thinking about. After all, could there be a worse moment than his first practice for a coach to fall on his face?

Mike and I arrive at the dressing room by seven thirty but we're not the first, not even the second. A couple of keeners are already getting ready as we walk in. I introduce myself and Mike, engage in some friendly small talk, then tape a handwritten sign on the dressing room door: *Team 5*. We won't know our real name and jersey colour until the league assigns us a sponsor.

Most of the team arrives by quarter to eight. Parents introduce kids, but few boys say anything more than hi. A few of the parents give me their name as well. Travis walks in and immediately recognizes me from soccer. "You coach hockey too?" he says. "You any good?"

"I don't know," I reply, being honest. "I've never done it before."

He smirks, clearly unimpressed. His mom ushers him to an open spot before he can say more. I spot a couple of dads' eyebrows raise when they hear I'm a rookie. Both quickly look away and occupy themselves with their kids' equipment. The room is quiet. I formally introduce myself and make my first announcement.

"I've passed around a clipboard with a form for you to fill out. I'd like to get the parents' first names and e-mail addresses. The names are for a team list I'll make up, and the e-mail is for sending out team notices."

As I finish, a dad hands me the clipboard, already complete. Scanning the list, I see everyone's here. Not even a day's notice and they all make it. I'm impressed.

By 8:05, everyone's ready and standing behind the end boards, waiting for the teams before us to finish. The buzzer sounds and they file off. But we wait as the Zamboni slides between the open doors at the other end of the rink. The kids watch quietly as it goes round and round, flooding the ice in six-foot swaths.

I hand Brad the stickhandling drills. He takes a look at the diagrams and quickly nods. "Looks simple enough," he says.

I give Sean the shooting drills and explain how each of us will man a station. "At ten minutes, I'll blow the whistle and the kids will rotate."

"Sounds good," says Sean.

Neither seems as excited about the station idea as I am.

A couple of kids fall stepping onto the ice, but I manage to negotiate the drop safely. I let the kids circle the rink a few times to loosen up, then blow my whistle and gather the team in our half of the ice. After explaining how things will run, I split them into the smaller groups, and take five with me. I run the skating station, because I doubt anyone else would want to. Besides, kids will happily practice shooting and stickhandling all day. There's a better chance they'll pay attention to skating if the guy explaining it is the coach.

After demonstrating the forward stride, I anxiously watch each boy give it a try. Travis skates low to the ice, knees deeply bent. He's a solid, powerful skater. Other coaches wanted to trade for him at the draft and I can see why. Braeden is the typical skinny little kid, skating on his ankles. He's not as bad as his dad claimed but he definitely needs work. Ryan's quick with a classic stride—there won't be much I can teach him. Most of the others are average—they start the stride late and end it early. Still, I'm pleased with the effort. Everyone tries to do it properly.

Between kids I glance at the other stations. They seem to be working. All fifteen kids are moving, not a goof-off to be found. I like it. When I sound the whistle, the rotation goes smoothly. It's like the kids want to move on and try what's next.

After thirty minutes, we start the three-on-twos. The kids listen attentively as I explain what we're doing. I assign positions based on where the boys will be playing in our first game. As before, the kids quickly go where they're told and the drill goes remarkably well. The kids who must wait do so patiently. A few of the forwards stand out from the rest. Justin is tall and stickhandles well. He looks like a good centre. Ryan uses his speed fearlessly to beat most of the bigger boys to the puck. Mike does well. I get the sense we'll be okay—no better, no worse than any other team.

Before I know it, the buzzer sounds and practice is over. On the way to the dressing room, one father introduces himself and says I ran a good practice. Another overhears and joins in, saying he too liked it, particularly the skating. A third pipes in from behind, adding it's smart to break the kids into smaller groups: "Isolates the troublemakers," he says with a wink. As a soccer coach, I never cared what parents thought. But today, I admit, I'm relieved. Good team, good parents.

Once everyone's in the dressing room, I tell them I'd normally have a package of written material, but I only got the team yesterday. Sean is silent, giving no indication the team used to be his. I explain my philosophy on teams, letting them know future practices will be more of what they saw today, individual skills for the first half hour, team skills to end.

"Looks like a good team T.J.," says Sean once the players have cleared out. "How about that Travis, huh?"

"Yeah, they look alright," echoes Brad. "Of course we won't know till we see them play. But one thing's for sure," he adds with a wink, "we're still undefeated."

THE GAMES BEGIN

The first hockey game of the season is always exciting, even if it's not your first time coaching. Players are eager to try out new equipment and to start playing games again. Parents want to see how their son fits in with the other boys on the ice. Even league officials are anxious to know what the teams look like, and whether or not they're evenly balanced.

It's ironic. Hockey-wise, it can easily be the worst game of the season. The coach hasn't had time to teach the boys anything, and players aren't even remotely used to each other. But many observers will decide if this is going to be a good or bad year based on how the team looks, first time out. As such, it's not a game you want to lose.

We play on Saturdays but we'll rotate venues and times all season. We start with a morning game—nine o'clock—at Twin Woods Arena, the second oldest rink in town. Built in the fifties, it makes use of every square foot. The building is not much bigger than the ice surface. Dressing rooms and a snack bar occupy one end; the garage for the Zamboni is at the other. The stands, only a few rows deep, flank one side of the ice, opposite the players' benches and penalty boxes. Hallways are short and narrow. Everything is packed tightly together.

Mike and I arrive at quarter after eight. While he heads to the dressing room I get an update from Rose. The team numbers have become names. We're the Cougars and we open the season against the Wildcats—the team we share our practice ice with. Rose hands me a bag full of sweaters and wishes me luck. The jerseys look good—royal blue with gold highlights. I take them back to the dressing room where kids have begun to arrive.

Rather than ask who wants which number, I simply hang them around the room. Fortunately, no one seems to care what number they get. Mike pulls number eight off a hook.

"Why'd you pick that one?" I ask.

"Cause I'm eight years old. Next year I'll pick nine."

I decide not to remind him he didn't wear seven last year or six the year before that.

While the kids get dressed, I distribute the handouts I've made for parents. On one I've listed each player and their parents' first names, address, phone number and the game they need to bring drinks for the team. I've combined the league's confusing game and practice schedules into one easy-to-read piece of paper. Lastly, I've made up a document entitled *Your Turn at Centre*. I figured giving everyone a chance was a good selling point for the team so I put it down in black and white. It may be controversial—no other team I know of has done it—but there'll be no backing down now.

Each parent glances over the handouts but I only get a reaction from one dad. On seeing the last document he immediately tells the entire room to get ready for a loss on the day his son plays centre.

Once everyone's ready with skates tied, I announce the lineup. At centre, I picked three boys I thought would make us competitive: Travis for his speed, Justin for the way he impressed me in practice and Will, who I know has good game sense. I put Mike on defence just to show everyone I'm not favouring my son; he'll take turns like everyone else. And I've told Mike he has to play like a true defenceman—he's supposed to set up goals, not score them. The rest of the kids' positions have been allocated based on a spreadsheet I prepared at home. I've laid out the first six weeks in a way that gives everyone a chance at all positions. I'll make notes on who does best where.

For my first pre-game talk, I give the boys a quick rundown on the fundamentals of their position. I deliberately keep it simple. Defencemen shoot the puck up the boards as fast as they can. Forwards pass the puck in front of the other team's net. That's it. Nothing else.

"So defencemen," I start, intending to see who was listening, "what was it you're supposed to do today?"

None of them move but Mike shoots his hand up instantly.

"Someone other than Mike . . . Joel."

Mike groans.

"Keep the puck away from your own net," he answers.

"That's right. Good answer. And what do you do with the puck once you get it? Where do you shoot it?"

"Up the boards," reply two others in unison.

"Good stuff." I turn to the forwards and with the same sort of prodding; they too repeat the one simple task that will form the basis of our strategy. Glancing around the room I suddenly notice Tommy and realize I forgot to mention our goalie. "Tommy," I improvise, "you know what to do, right? Just like in practice—challenge those shooters."

Tommy nods and there's a brief silence. I also forgot to think of an ending. "Okay boys," I announce, "let's go have some fun."

There's a split second pause before they realize that's their cue to head for the ice. They rise together and trudge out of the room, single file.

"Should I have led them in a cheer?" I ask Brad on our way out. "They're so quiet."

"I don't think it matters," he replies. "Some do, some don't."

On the ice, we use the same warm-up Joe's coach uses. Each game, one kid shoots on the goalie while the others skate around. Since we only have three minutes, it eliminates confusion. Each kid will get a turn shooting. This week it'll be number two, next week number three and so on.

The buzzer sounds to signal the game is about to begin. Rose wants the teams to shake hands before the game. Seeing them line up at centre ice reminds me that the rationale for not doing it after the game comes from Rep hockey—too many fist fights.

The rink quiets as the referee puts his hand in the air, calling the players to centre ice. He checks with each goalie to ensure they're ready and then drops the puck. We're underway.

It would be great to say the boys immediately begin skating and passing like a well-oiled machine, but they don't. It's just too early. The kids are excited but don't know how to play. It's nowhere near a team game. The skater with the puck takes it as far as he can before someone takes it away. Then that boy repeats the pattern. Possession changes constantly. Scoring chances are few and far between.

The kids on the bench are quiet. It's strange. They watch the play but there's no cheering, no nothing. Ten kids just watch intently, silently.

As for the players on the ice, I try to help them by repeating the two things we talked about in the dressing room. "Shoot it up the boards," I yell, when our defencemen have the puck. "Pass it out front," I shout to the forwards. I can't tell if they hear me or not, but regardless, I know the boys on the bench do. They'll be out soon enough.

It doesn't take long for Brad to prove I couldn't have made a better choice for an assistant. "Hey Kevin," he says, putting his hand on the boy's shoulder pad as he comes off the ice. "You know how you've been staying back when one of our players takes the puck into the other team's zone? Well, sometimes that's a good idea, but you know what I'd like you to try next? What if you try to stay even with the other forwards as they're going in, and let our defence trail the play. You think you could do that?" His tone is friendly and respectful.

Kevin nods without hesitation. A couple of shifts later Kevin is still hanging back, but Brad simply reminds him how they agreed to try a new way of playing. The easy, non-threatening tone Brad uses with Kevin is exactly the way I'd like a coach to speak to my son. I'm impressed.

The Wildcats get a scoring chance late in the first period. One of their players shoots from the left faceoff circle. Tommy makes the save, but the rebound goes to the opposite side of the net where one of their players is standing alone. He taps it in for a one-nothing lead. In the second period we get a chance of our own. Mike lifts the puck high in the air to send Will in on a breakaway. He shoots, he misses. Game on.

Early in the third, Turner takes a spot on the bench, and after a brief pause, looks over at me. "Hey Coach," he says.

I realize it's the first time anyone's called me coach at a hockey rink. I like it. "Hey Turner. What's up?"

He diverts his eyes to the ice and mumbles something in a low voice. Between his mouth guard and face mask, I haven't a clue what he said. I ask him to repeat it but still can't make out the words. Finally, on the third try, he takes off his glove, pulls out his mouthguard and says: "I elbowed a guy."

My first inclination is to tell him to say three Hail Mary's and forget it, but the look on his face is serious. "Really?" I ask. "I didn't see anything."

"Yeah," he assures me, frowning soberly, "I elbowed him."

"Well, elbowing is definitely serious but . . . Wait a minute,

Turner, are you absolutely sure you elbowed a guy? I was watching you and I didn't see anything."

"Remember when I was down in the crease?"

"Yeah."

"The guy kicked me. So when I was getting up, I elbowed him."

"Oh. I see. Well, the ref probably thought he'd let you off this time because it all came out kind of even. Guess you got away with one."

Turner smiles, his eyes lighting up. "Yeah, guess I got away with one."

A few minutes later, we pick up a rebound and ring it off the post. The goalie smothers the puck. We're still behind. With a minute and a half left, I pull the goalie, mainly to let parents and kids know I'm the kind of coach who tries to win. We get all of one shot and it's a weak one. Our first game ends in a one-nothing loss.

"So much for our undefeated streak," I say to Brad on the way back to the dressing room.

"Don't worry T.J.," he replies. "It was bound to end sooner or later."

In the dressing room afterward, the kids are neither up nor down. I tell them we had our chances but sometimes things don't work out. The shot that hit the post could easily have been a goal. And we definitely had more shots. The boys seem to buy it. After all, it is the truth. A few echo my comments to the player sitting next to them. We lost but there doesn't seem to be any ill effect.

On the drive home, I'm feeling much the same as the boys. I would have preferred to win but, on balance, I thought we were better. If I had to pick which team I'd rather coach, it would be ours.

Later, I realize there's a silver lining I hadn't thought of. As convenor, Rose must decide whether or not to move players around to balance the league. Four teams won today; four lost. If she moves anyone, it will have to come from a winner. So it looks like we're a good team that just guaranteed it would remain intact.

All in all, it seems like a fine start. We've got talent, appreciative parents and circumstance has smiled on us. Our next practice is tomorrow and it's already planned. I still have to finalize my assistant coaches and draft a team budget, but so far, coaching a boys' hockey team seems a lot easier than I thought it would be. I almost wonder what could possibly go wrong.

 **REALITY SETS IN**

With our first game in the books, I need to resolve the coaching situation, specifically, George. Despite a couple of reminders, Sean still hasn't called Rose to officially resign. That bugs me. Is he waiting until I name him assistant coach? That's not fair.

The opposition to George also bothers me. I know him better than any of those who have spoken against him. To me, the story that says the most about the man happened two years earlier when I was running a soccer practice. I'd undergone arthroscopic surgery on my knee the week before, and was limping badly.

"T.J., should you be doing this?" he asked.

"Ah, it's not as bad as it looks," I replied in typical man-style. "I'll be fine."

But the very first drill was one the boys had never done before. Soccer balls were flying everywhere. With a huge bandage wrapped around my knee, I hobbled after each one, trying to keep the drill going. At least twelve different parents watched. No one said a thing. George must've thought it looked ridiculous.

"Brenda, Joel, get out there," he said to his daughter and son playing beside the practice field. "T.J. needs help. You get the balls and make sure he doesn't do any more running, okay?"

They did and, boy, I appreciated it. It's something I've never forgotten. Further, my experience in life has been entirely consistent—it's the actions, not the words, which make the man. So how can I turn down a man who takes the initiative to help someone?

No, my mind's made up. If George has rough edges then the kids and parents will just have to deal with them—he's going to be our assistant coach. I call him Saturday afternoon to let him know. He's ecstatic.

"Can I bring anything to practice? Pucks, water bottles, whatever you need; I got it all."

"Actually, if you have a set of water bottles, that'd be great."

"Sure, no problem," he replies. "This'll be fun."

I call up Sean to let him know I've picked a friend of mine to assist. "He really wants to coach but the league won't give him a team," I explain. "He figures if he's an assistant this year, he can get his own team next year." Sean understands and promises to officially resign.

Sunday's practice is at IceTime, a relatively new building with four rinks downstairs and a full restaurant and viewing area upstairs. This time Mike and I are the first in the dressing room—something he's not crazy about since he's a fast dresser and doesn't need the extra time. Sean and Patrick arrive next. Sean doesn't even mention the coaching. Instead we chat about the game.

As Sean talks, Patrick's behind him, emptying his hockey bag. Unconventionally. Piece by piece, he throws his equipment high in the air. My eyes can't help following the elbow and shoulder pads flying around the room. Sean starts talking about his team from last year while I try not to think about what Patrick will do with his jock strap. Fortunately, he doesn't get there. When he grabs his hockey pants, he drapes them over his head and starts running around the room yelling, "Who turned out the lights? Who turned out the lights?" Mike can't contain himself and bursts out laughing.

"Patrick!" shouts Sean, finally acknowledging what's going on. "Smarten up." Then he turns to me again. "Patrick has a bit of a focus problem," he explains.

Twenty minutes later, the boys are dressed and waiting by the glass. The buzzer sounds and we take to the ice. As soon as I step out, I notice two players behaving oddly at the blue line. Patrick and his alleged best friend, Simon, are punching each other as they skate their warm up. It's something I've never seen before—kind of a stride-punch combination.

"Guys, what're you doing?" I ask, catching up to them.

"He started it," says Simon.

"No I didn't. He started it," claims Patrick.

"Yeah, well I'm going to end it," I announce in my sternest voice. Before I complete the threat, Patrick skates off in another direction.

I take the pucks to our end, blow my whistle and we start the stations. It doesn't take long to see the George decision was the right one. After leaving George with five boys to work on stickhandling, I overhear him say, " . . . but before we do that, I'm going to teach you how to fight. Come on!"

I turn around to see five little kids ganging up on a bear-sized man, all laughing and screaming as they play fight near the side boards. "Okay, okay, enough already," he says in short order. "Let's see if you know how to stickhandle."

Once we've finished the stations, we divide the team in two for a game I know they'll like: one-on-one keep away. The first two players begin the game inside the faceoff circles. The rest of the kids stand outside the "ring," ready to pass the puck back, should one of the two combatants lose control. It goes well but a few minutes later, Patrick's flat on his back, making imaginary snow angels on the ice. I look into the stands for Sean but he's preoccupied, talking with one of the other parents. With Patrick down, a couple of other kids start firing pucks into the boards as they wait their turn. Suddenly, the boys don't seem so eager to learn.

"Come on Patrick, up you go," I say, pulling him to his feet. Predictably, he lets his legs buckle the first two times, but eventually stands up and rejoins the game. When the buzzer sounds to end the practice. I'm grateful.

Reflecting on it later, this practice felt more like work than the last one. Brad, George and I were the only dads on the ice. No less than eight others have volunteered to help but I've yet to enlist anyone. Too many times I've seen five or six dads on the ice with nothing to do. They're usually as bad as their kids. In no time, they're shooting pucks around, skating at top speed and distracting the players. However, if things continue as they were today, we'll need at least one more adult, just as a babysitter.

Fortunately, the next day when I'm picking up Mike and Joe from school, I run into Will's dad. We've known each other for a couple of years so we begin to chat briefly about hockey. "Travis' father still plays," he replies, on hearing my helper dilemma. "He's pretty good. Travis seems to focus more when his dad's on the ice."

That caught my attention. Focus had been Travis' problem in soccer. He had talent, but was more interested in fooling around. It hadn't surfaced in hockey yet, but the season was young. Once home, I send Travis' dad, Dave, an e-mail asking if he'd like to come out to our next practice. I glance at the schedule and cringe, it's our worst time: six o'clock next Wednesday morning.

"Don't worry about it," Dave replies. "I'm up anyway. And I'd love to come out with the boys. It's a great game and a privilege to teach it to youngsters."

Did he say privilege? Wow. Maybe he can look after Patrick.

That night I tackle what other coaches say is the worst part of the job—the team budget. The league provides the elements of a basic hockey experience—one game and one half-ice practice every week. But in the Gold division, many parents look for more: tournaments, exhibition games, extra practices, team clothing, names on the jerseys, etc. It all has a cost. The coach must decide how many extras he wants to go for. Then he has to find the money. Usually it comes from the parents.

The first time I was asked to contribute extra money to a team, I didn't appreciate it. I felt the registration fee of $350 was steep enough. I'm used to it now, but each year I wonder where the money goes. A coach is entitled to make these decisions, but I'm not comfortable telling people they must contribute an amount of money because I say so. Thinking it over gives me a better idea—let the parents decide for themselves.

I draft a survey asking parents to vote on a myriad of hockey extras. I'm able to provide cost estimates based on the league's coaching manual. Now it'll be simple—whatever the majority wants, they'll get. And they'll know what it costs, up front.

This Saturday, our game is at IceTime. It's much later—6:10 P.M. In contrast to the cold mornings at Twin Woods, the upstairs viewing area ensures that evenings at IceTime will be warm, at least for the spectators.

We're missing Justin and Luke, both visiting relatives out of town. The league stipulates that when you're short two players, you must play four defencemen instead of six. This means those four players get more ice time than anyone else. I could pick four at random but, after losing the first game, I do the same thing other teams do in this situation: go with four of our best. I'll keep Mike on defence, as well as Turner, Ryan and Joel. That way, we'll have two good players on the ice at all times.

I'm also trying something a little hokey, calling this a "heads up" game. At practice, we tried to teach the kids to shoot and stickhandle with their heads up. So today, any boy who does it during the game gets a stick of licorice.

We're playing the Giants, coached by two men I know well. They each have older boys who've been on Joe's soccer teams. We've shared laughs and won some trophies. However, when it comes to hockey, their experience is a little intimidating. One played Junior A, winning an Ontario championship. The other is a sports fanatic who's great at teasing and cajoling the best out of young kids. Together, they coached two teams last year. Both won championships. They claim they've tried to get my sons on their teams, but never have. At the draft, the convenor paid more attention to them than anyone else. As it ended, the fanatic announced I had the best team. Then he threw down the gauntlet: "Doesn't mean you'll have the best team at the end though."

Before the game, I looked over the Giants' roster. I use a very simple test to assess talent—if I recognize a kid's name I know he's good. Otherwise, I wouldn't have remembered him. There's no one on the Giants' roster I recall. No question the coaches are good, but two weeks isn't enough time to make an impact. This should be our first win of the season.

While the kids get dressed, I tell parents I've heard from the organizer of a Select tournament in Toronto that sounds pretty good. I explain the difference between House League and Select, so they know our opponents will most likely be all-star teams. Then I spell out my rationale for wanting to play at the Select level. We play in a Gold House League. Our team is stronger than regular House League teams. From a hockey standpoint, the boys would get much more out of a tight game they lost, than a game they won easily. A few parents nod in agreement.

For the pre-game talk, I give the boys the same instructions as last week. Defencemen, shoot the puck up the boards. Forwards, get the puck in front of the other team's net. That's it. Do those two things and we'll be fine. Once again, the boys head to the ice in silence.

After completing our three-minute warm-up the boys find

their positions, and the puck drops. From a brief scramble at centre ice, we shoot the puck into their end. Turner is first to the puck and centres it. Travis shoots. It's in. Just like that.

"Alright!" I scream. We've scored our first goal of the season in the very first minute of the game. We're finally on our way. Travis leads his teammates back to our bench for a high-five skate by. One by one, the boys on the ice slap the gloves of the boys on the bench. Save for Patrick. He's put his own spin on the celebration. Instead of slapping the gloves, he tries to punch each face mask.

"Patrick," I say firmly, "Smarten up."

Patrick merely shrugs and looks back on the ice. The five players skate to centre for the faceoff. The puck drops again. As soon as it hits the ice, the sports fanatic's son takes it all the way to our net, finishing with a high wrist shot into the mesh. Tie game. Just like that.

Then, in case we hadn't noticed, the same boy does the same thing again. And four minutes after that, a Giant centreing pass hits Turner's skate and ricochets into our net. The score's three-one. I tell Mike to forget what I said about playing back. If he sees an opening, take it.

Two shifts later, Mike gets his chance. He picks up the puck near our blue line, dekes one, then two Giants, and streaks down the left side of the ice. With one more to beat, Mike looks to have the angle. The whistle sounds. I immediately look for the ref, wondering why on earth he stopped the play. Then I see. Well behind the play, Patrick is slumped on the ice. I look at Brad. "What happened?"

Brad shrugs. "I didn't see anything."

We wait as the ref helps Patrick to his feet. Once up, players on both teams slap their sticks on the ice—a ritual performed to help the injured player feel better. The ref steers Patrick toward the bench but before he arrives, Patrick decides he's okay after all. He can continue playing. Mike is standing by the boards, the puck still on his stick. It doesn't take a genius to know what he's thinking.

The players skate back into position. The faceoff is in the Giants' zone but the scoring chance is lost and play continues without any meaningful shots.

In the second period the game takes on a different tone. Virtually every shift is played between the Giants' blue line and our goal line. They skate into our end looking for a shot, but our defence thwart most of their attempts, and shoot it up the boards. Unfortunately, the Giants' defencemen are first to the puck and pass it right back to their forwards. They re-enter our zone, and occasionally get a shot before we clear it. The process repeats itself, again and again. Still, Tommy's playing well and we manage to hold them off the scoresheet despite the play advantage.

Meanwhile, Patrick has gone down three more times. Brad has been out twice to help him, but on the third lets the ref handle it. Each time Patrick rises to the sound of sticks slapping the ice, all eyes focused on him. Each time, miracle of miracles, Patrick is able to overcome his injury and continue. Early in the third period he goes down for the fifth time.

"Bring him off," I say to Brad who nods in agreement. He opens the gate, heads out on the ice, and returns with Patrick who hobbles onto our bench.

"Hey Patrick. You okay buddy?" I ask in my most sympathetic voice.

"No. It really hurts."

"I'll bet. You know what? I think we're going to keep you off for the rest of the game, just to be safe."

"What!" he screams in disbelief.

"Patrick, injuries are serious. I don't want to risk getting you hurt. I think it's best if you sit out the rest of the game."

"No, it's okay. I think it's better now."

"Well I want to be sure. In fact, guys," I announce to the bench, "from now on, whenever someone gets injured, we'll sit them off a shift, just to make sure they're okay. We want to have fun but we have to be safe. Right?"

"I'm fine. I want to play," continues Patrick.

A few players smile, as if they weren't fooled any more than I was. While Patrick carries on asserting his good health, I watch the play.

It's not getting any better. I've now told all four defencemen to rush the puck if they see an opening, but this is a good old-fashioned butt kicking. The Giants are all over us. And the sports fanatic's son is having a field day. A few minutes into the third, he completes his hat trick, intercepting a pass at our blue line and taking it in all alone. After the teams exchange goals he notches his fourth to make it a six-two rout. As the seconds tick down, there can be no argument the score is fair. If anything, they should've beaten us by more. As a final insult, in the last minute of play, Mike is shoved headfirst into the boards and stays down. It turns out his shoulder takes the brunt of the impact, but the very first injury under our new rule is my own son's. The thumping is complete.

On the way to the dressing room, I shake hands with the two coaches. "Tough game," says the ex-Junior A player, chuckling.

"Yeah. Good luck with your team," says the sports fanatic, laughing under his breath.

In all my years coaching soccer, I've never laughed at an opposing coach. After two games in hockey, guys I know are making fun of me.

I'm not looking forward to the dressing room. As I approach, the parents are already arriving. Raised eyebrows, courteous smiles. The looks say it all: Don't worry. We know you're a nice guy. The important thing is the boys are having fun.

Absolutely. Kids love to lose. That's when they have the most fun. The dressing room is silent as I walk in. I know I should say something but I have no idea what. "Well boys, some days it'll go our way and some days it won't." The kids undress as fast as they can. "Today, it didn't." I try to lead the team in three cheers, but participation is so woeful a few of the parents laugh. "Come on guys, it's not that bad."

But it is. There's no question our bubble has burst. Good teams don't get killed the way we did. I hand out the sticks of licorice to everyone, ignoring the pre-game deal, hoping it will make the boys feel better. But it's useless. No one, least of all a player, could be under any illusion after that. We lost because the other team was better. Period. And I'm the coach—the one who wanted to give these kids the perfect season. Right. So now what?

# THE TRUTH ABOUT THE DRAFT

I don't know what real hockey coaches do after a big loss, but I pour myself a glass of red wine and set my recliner back full tilt. The Leafs game is on and thankfully I'm alone. The boys are playing hockey in the basement, my daughter's out babysitting and my wife is catching up on her invoicing for work.

Losses always bug me, but usually I can figure out why and identify something to work on in practice, a hope for the future. Not this time. They killed us. No ifs, ands or buts. The Giants were the better team and it wasn't even close. We can work on whatever we want but they'll still be better. How did this happen? On paper, I thought we were supposed to be the stronger team, or at least even. I thought we were good.

I run upstairs to look through my hockey file. I want to know more about these Giants and why they beat us so easily. First I recheck the team list, but recognize only a few of the names, and no one I'd call a real star. So who are these others?

Then I turn to last year's coaches' ratings, given to us at the draft. Sixteen pages stapled together—eight for Gold and eight for Silver. Each coach rated every boy on his team in ten different categories. Coaches spend a lot of time on this and one thing's for sure: they all know who their best players are. I search the lists for our players to see what last year's coaches thought of them. The results surprise me.

First, no less than seven of the boys on our team played in the Silver division last year—almost half our team. I'd heard they promoted thirty boys into the eight teams in Gold division. That works out to three or four per team. So why do we have twice that many?

Even worse, last year's coaches recommended that three of our players stay in Silver. Two more were ranked as borderline—the coach wasn't sure whether or not to recommend them for Gold. Four of these boys played forward today. Small wonder we didn't have much of an attack.

I check out the other teams to see how we compare. An hour later, I've found out. The Giants are good but according to last year's coaches, only third best. We're dead last. Once you get past our top players, the drop-off is steep. No other team has as many players rated as low as ours.

It's frustrating. Based on that silly skate-around they held a month ago, our boys are equal to any other team. But according to the coaches who saw players every week in game situations, we're going to get killed.

Dressing room images from earlier today come flooding back: kids, looking away from me, hurriedly getting dressed, not saying a word; the parents with brave attempts at smiles. How will they feel if we keep losing? Five in a row? Ten in a row? Last year a team managed just one win all season. Six kids quit the team. Could that happen to us? To me?

What about Mike? How would he handle a losing season? With his dad as coach, it wouldn't be pretty. I'd wanted a perfect season. This could be a nightmare.

The most frustrating thing is that I'd objected when the other coaches decided to select teams based on a skate-around. I suggested using the coaches' ratings from last year. But no, I was the new kid on the block. The voices of experience knew better.

Fortunately, the league doesn't want a losing team any more than kids or coaches do. One of the primary roles of the convenor is to ensure the teams are balanced, so that each kid has more or less the same chance to win a hockey game. Rose has no kids or grandkids in the league—nothing to sway her opinion. She knows we've lost two in a row, but I doubt she's compared the teams using last year's coach's ratings. Should I do it for her?

It's not as simple as wanting to win. I've been through this in soccer and it isn't fun. To balance us, they'll need to take one, two or three players off our team. Naturally, they'll pick the weakest. Kids aren't stupid. The ones who move know why. It's not something they'll feel good about. What if they ask me to pick the kids? So much for Mr. Nice Guy.

A second reality bugs me too. Balancing almost never works. I don't know why, since intuitively, you think it should work. But every time I've seen it done, the upgraded team still finishes last. What if I ask to be balanced and at the end of the season we're still in last place? I'll have upset a few eight-year-olds for nothing.

And what about coaching? I did this because I believed I could help these kids. So what am I saying now—I can only help kids who are already good? That's not right.

Our next practice is a good one. For some reason, the team is up. The stations go well and during the teamwork drills, the passes connect. It's tough watching the weaker kids, wondering if we'll lose one or two. They all have hockey ability. It's not as if they're not trying, or not thinking. Even the weakest kid on the team impresses me in some way. I know I can help them. And Patrick participates in all the drills without incident.

Dave takes the shooting station and once again, it's obvious he's the right man for the job. He gets down on one knee, looks the kids in the eye and explains the drill. Then he demonstrates and asks if they understand. Without question we have a good group of coaches.

In the dressing room, after the kids have left, Brad asks if there's been any talk of balancing. I haven't been able to bring myself to call the convenor.

"What would you think if we didn't balance," I ask, "and just go with the players we have? I know we've lost both games but, maybe we can turn it around."

The room is silent.

"I can tell you one thing," says George, after a pause, "we definitely have the three worst kids in the league."

"That's for sure," echoes Dave. "The difference between our top and bottom players is huge. They can't even skate." The look on his face is one of disbelief. I know he's given Travis a lot of extra instruction. I get the impression he can't understand why other parents wouldn't do the same.

"I must admit," chimes in Brad, "you always get one or two kids you have to work with, but we've got more than a few. I have no idea how some of these guys made Gold."

It's hard to argue. Neither team we've played has the disparity we have, and on paper, what they're saying is true. In fact, it's the same thing each of those player's coaches said last year. But I want to play devil's advocate a little longer.

"We know they'll get better. And we have Travis, Mike and Joel. They have to be three of the best players in the league. We can split them up, make sure one's out there all the time."

"Exactly," replies George. "So all the other teams have to do is shut down one player and it's game over. You want your kid double-teamed all season? He'll be hacked to death. T.J., I'll do whatever you want, but I'm telling you, unless we get rid of at least one of our weaker players, we won't win a game till Christmas."

Christmas. That's when I was hoping to enter the Select tournament. Playing all-star teams from other house leagues. If we can't win a game in our league, what will happen there?

"I don't see what the big deal is," claims Brad. "Tell Rose we don't need anyone's best player. Just give us someone who can skate."

"Yeah," adds Dave. "They should've been spreading these guys around anyway. You can't put all the lousy players on one team."

"Okay," I announce, relenting. "I'll give her a call and see what she thinks."

On the drive home, I can't resist asking Mike if he thinks we can win with this team.

"Yeah," he replies, abruptly. His tone suggests he's insulted I would even ask such a question.

"Do you think we can win a lot of games?"

"Will I get to play forward?"

"Mike, you're only playing defence to show the parents I'm not the kind of coach who puts his son on centre all the time. Like I said, we take turns."

He nods, then looks out the window. There's silence, as if he's forgotten the question. Clearly one of us takes this far more seriously than the other.

"So you think we can win some games, even though we've got these guys who can't skate?" I ask, watching his response through the rear view mirror.

"Yeah," he says calmly. He's still looking out the window.

"Do you think we can win the championship?"

This time there's no response, even though at 7:22 A.M. on a weekday morning there is absolutely nothing happening outside his window.

"Mike, do you think we can win the championship?"

"I don't know," he replies, dismissively.

There is no point continuing this conversation. And now I'm wondering if kids even care who wins the championship. Certainly my kid doesn't. But the votes are in. Coaches say balance, conscience says don't and my kid says everything will be fine—all I have to do is open his cage.

I call the convenor later that morning. The conversation is short but gratifying since Rose seems to be a kindred spirit. The bottom line is she wants to see my analysis. She claims she never liked the way the teams were put together in the first place and knew from the start it wouldn't work. Because the coaches insisted, she allowed it. She doesn't want to move kids but feels she has no choice. She'll wait one more game, and then make her decision. I'm impressed.

As I hang up, I feel it's only a matter of time. Anyone looking at that analysis will see how uneven the teams are. I wonder if we'll get one, two or three players. I'd prefer a package, even if it means giving up a strong player. That way, no one feels singled out. I wonder if Rose has thought of handling it that way. I'll suggest it Saturday.

I'm feeling better now. Moving a group of kids to balance the league should be easy to do. The kids won't be bothered and parents will appreciate it. We're not the only weak team. According to my analysis, two teams got the short end of the stick at the draft. This will help them both and make thirty-two kids happier.

I check the schedule to see who our lucky opponent will be this weekend. My heart sinks. It's the other weakest team in the league. Later in the season this might be good news—a chance to win. But Rose said she'd balance after this game. One of us will win. The first rule of convening is: winning teams never get balanced. So the winner remains the weakest team in the league. It could be their last victory for a long time.

To make matters worse, the two strongest teams will play each other. The same will hold, only in reverse. One of them will lose and appear not so strong after all. That team will remain intact. In their case, it could be their last loss of the season. I shake my head in disbelief—only in minor sports could the losers be better off than the winners, at least this weekend.

For a brief moment I think about calling Rose and explaining the situation. No, I'm not saying anything more. I already feel like a schmuck for saying as much as I have. This is kids hockey—a bunch of eight-year-olds playing a game. Whatever happens, happens. I'm forty-two years old. Life isn't perfect. I'll try to help these kids but if the cards don't turn in our favour, too bad.

For all my good intentions, I'm beginning to feel like an idiot. In trying to make this an idyllic year, I've lost track of the whole reason we're doing this.

Every Saturday a group of kids come together to play a game. It may be organized but it's just a game. It's not going to make or break anyone's life. You play games because they're fun and you always try your hardest to win. So this Saturday, that's what we're going to do.

OPENING CAGES

The complaint I've heard most often about hockey coaches is they feature their son as the starting centre. I didn't want anyone criticizing me for that, but unfortunately, it did pose a problem. Every coach Mike's had, eventually puts him at centre, and usually, to start the game. With his speed, passing ability and strong two-way play, the truth is, he's a natural.

I figured the best way to avoid the issue was to make Mike the last to play forward and the last to start a game. My intentions may have been noble but I could see now I overdid it.

For starters, immediately following our loss to the Giants, one of the parents asked me if I could please put Mike on forward. They felt it was obvious he belonged there and the team needed him. When I explained my rationale and desire to be fair, the parent smiled politely and concluded the discussion with an abrupt "So he'll be on forward then?"

Secondly, I'd completely overlooked the fact that the individual bearing the cross was not a forty-two-year-old man concerned with his image. Instead, it was an eight-year-old boy no different from any other. He wanted to be on the ice when the game started and he wanted to play forward.

So on Friday night, while eating dinner and listening patiently to his siblings review the highs and lows of their day, Mike suddenly interrupts the conversation. "Am I playing forward this week?" he asks, looking straight at me.

"I think so."

"Really?" His eyes widen.

"You've played defence twice. It's your turn to play forward."

"Do I get to start?"

"Yup. The forwards are you, Will and Turner."

Mike immediately returns to his dinner and says nothing more. But he has the distinct air of someone who senses things are about to fall into place and doesn't want to do anything that might tempt the gods.

On Saturday morning, Mike's up early and is ready before it's time to leave. We're back at Twin Woods, playing the Huskies. It's a twenty-minute ride to the rink, long enough for the player to remind the coach whose line is on first, and which position he was promised.

We're one of the first in the dressing room and Mike quickly gets ready. Turner arrives and Mike motions him over. "Guess who's on first?" he asks with a big smile.

Turner shrugs.

"You, me and Will. With Tommy and Kevin on defence. Can you believe we finally get to start a game?"

Turner smiles in a way that says he's happy Mike's happy, but isn't sure what the big deal is.

The pre-game talk is identical to last week, short and simple. Once again, the boys file out of the dressing room, with little sign of emotion. But when the ref raises his hand in the air to signal the opening faceoff, Mike races into position.

The puck drops. Before either centre can get a stick on it, Mike swoops in from the wing and takes off, splitting the defence on his way to the net. When he reaches the hash marks, he shoots. The puck sails over the crossbar and crashes into the glass. Without a pause, he curls behind the net, retrieves it and passes out front to Turner. Their goalie saves the shot but Mike slams home the rebound. Our bench roars. I look at the clock. Eighteen seconds.

Mike sprints to the bench, leading his line for the celebratory high-fives. "Good hustle everyone," I yell as the boys return to centre for the faceoff. The rest of the two-minute shift is spent entirely in the Huskies' zone. Mike and Turner take several more shots but none get through. Still, there's a noticeable difference on our bench. For the first time, the boys are animated, cheering their teammates.

This week Travis takes his turn on defence, something he claims he "sucks at." Soon after his line takes to the ice, he's given a chance to prove it. A Huskies' forward takes a puck off the boards and quickly skates in on him. Travis calmly sweeps the puck off his stick and shoots it back up the ice.

"Alright Travis!" I yell, thinking he could use the encouragement. He gives no sign he heard me and, for the rest of the game, gives no sign he needs any encouragement. Shift after shift, Travis proves he definitely does not suck at defence. He utilizes his toughness to challenge any opponent who comes near, and his shot to rifle pucks out of our zone. Travis looks better on defence than he has on forward.

Mike leaves little doubt where he belongs. He scores on three of his five shifts. Watching him seems to inspire the others. It's like we're a brand new team. One that tries its hardest. We're the best in all three periods and fully deserve our six-two win. In the dressing room after, the boys are euphoric: yelling, shouting, and laughing.

While the boys get dressed, I join Rose back in the rink, watching the next game. She congratulates me on our win and says we looked good. I ask about balancing but she wants time to think it over. She says my analysis will help.

On the drive home, Mike chatters non-stop, going over play after play. I must confess, I feel better too. It's one of those things you hate to admit publicly, but the world is a much better place after a win.

Monday and Tuesday pass without any news from Rose. On Wednesday, I call her. She has decided to move players around, but none from our team. As expected, the team we beat, picked up two players—one from the team that won the battle of the best, and another from the Giants who had just won their third straight. So according to last year's coaches, we'll be the weakest team in the league.

For some reason it doesn't bother me. Whether it's the afterglow of winning or relief at not having to tell a kid they've been traded, I'm not sure. But at the end of the day, we have good coaches, and we're working on skills. We should be okay.

Practice falls on Friday night and the kids return to being attentive. As usual, it's skating, stickhandling and shooting for the first half hour, a team situation to finish. George says we're the only team running their practice this way and calls it unconventional. But the kids enjoy it. The drills are simple and never the same. They get ten minutes of power skating and twenty minutes with a puck. In their minds, I'm sure the team situation is like a mini-scrimmage. Small wonder they like it. Tonight, I notice a subtle difference from practices past. Whether it's last week's victory or simply the fact they've been together a month, they're starting to talk to each other.

Our next game is late Saturday afternoon at IceTime against the Hawks, the team that won the battle of the best. Even though they lost a player, on paper, they still look stronger than any other. I recognize several of their players' names and all are good athletes. The boy they lost is good, but I wouldn't have rated him any higher than fourth or fifth best. No question, this should be our toughest game yet.

My schedule of when kids would play centre deliberately slotted Mike, Ryan and Joel to take their turn against the Hawks. I figured three good centres might give us a fighting chance. Unfortunately, Travis' family picked this weekend to close their cottage, so we're going to have to make do without him.

"Defencemen," I shout in the dressing room once everyone's ready, "in our game last week, what did we do better than the other team?"

"Score," yells one.

"That's true. But I was thinking of something our defence did. And they did it a lot better than the other team."

The room is quiet. All I'm getting are blank stares.

"Remember? Before the game we said we were going to do something with the puck when it was in our end? What?"

Suddenly Braeden fires his hand into the air. "Shoot it up the boards," he says, confidently.

"That's right. And what're we going to do today?"

"Shoot it up the boards," says another, calmly, as if I'd just asked a stupid question.

"That's right. And you know what? We're going to be the best in the league at shooting the puck up the boards. 'Cause that's what the good teams do. Even in the NHL. When the puck is in their end, they shoot it up the boards. Think we can do it?"

"Yeah!" they scream.

Then I turn to the forwards and ask them what they should be doing. Mike's hand goes up in a flash, but I want to make sure someone else knows. "Ryan."

"Get the puck in front of their net?" he replies with a crinkled brow. Apparently he's only half sure.

"That's right. Think you can do it?"

Ryan and a few others nod. I wonder if I should be trying to stir them up more. It's not really my style but they're surprisingly quiet for boys who are about to play hockey. "Okay, so that's what we're going to do. Shoot the puck up the boards when it's in our end; pass it in front of the net when it's in theirs." The boys are all looking at me calmly, quietly. Suddenly I feel as mild mannered as they are. I just can't bring myself to lead eight-year-olds in a cheer. Instead, I end with a simple "let's go have some fun," as enthusiastically as I can make it.

Watching the two teams go through their warm-up, it's easy to see a difference. And unnerving. The Hawks are bigger and faster. A casual observer might think we play in two different leagues.

The ref calls the teams to centre. Seconds after the puck drops, three Hawks are in our zone, chasing the puck. Braeden, true to his word, picks up the puck and fires it off the boards toward the Hawk end. Our guys give chase. Unfortunately, all of our guys give chase. And when the Hawk defence shoots the puck back, it goes straight to their centre waiting alone, behind the play. He takes off, and is clearly much faster than anyone chasing him. Tommy stops his shot but the second guy to the net is another Hawk. He shoots high to make it one-nothing.

Two minutes later, their lead doubles on a similar play. One of the bigger Hawks intercepts a pass in the neutral zone and simply outskates our players to the net. He too shoots high into the mesh on Tommy's stick side. Two shifts, two goals.

"Come on guys, we can do better. Remember, shoot it out of our end and pass it in front of their net. Let's go."

On the very next shift, we do exactly that. Kevin fires the puck off the boards, Joel picks it up and skates into the Hawks end. Their defenceman knocks it off his stick but Joel is first to the puck and passes out front. Connor is there and shoots it by their goalie. We're on the board.

The very next shift, Will, Mike and Turner force the play in the Hawks' end. This time it's Turner who centres the puck and Mike bangs it home. Amazingly, we're tied two-two. On the fifth and last shift of the period, Ryan's line holds the Hawks at bay, breaking up plays before they get close to our net.

The second period sees a clear trend developing. The Hawks speed into our zone, only to have one of our players intercept a pass or knock the puck off their sticks. The minute we have the puck, it's cleared wide, up the boards, just as we talked about. The Hawks are faster and carrying the puck more than we are, but they're not getting many shots.

Mike and Turner are playing well. Both have the same tenacity and they're starting to work together—one pressing on the right while the other covers the left. Midway through the second, it pays off. Turner intercepts a Hawk pass and fires. Mike pounces on the rebound. It's three-two us.

The Hawks roar back and this time we have trouble stopping them. On the next two shifts they get no fewer than eight shots. Tommy stops them all, but if this keeps up, it's only a matter of time before they score.

Mike and Turner are up next. I put my arm on Mike's shoulder and my head between the two of them. "Guys, we really need a good shift. You two are better than they are. I need you to really go for it, okay?"

"Sure coach," says Turner. His tone surprises me. Like we're at the breakfast table and I've asked him to pass the sugar. No problem. Want the milk too?

The buzzer sounds and the two skate into position: Mike at centre, Turner on right. The puck drops. Immediately, it's as if the teams traded sweaters. We're all over them and they're chasing us. For the first minute their goalie is equal to the task, but early in the second, Mike takes a feed from Turner, dekes two Hawks, and lifts the puck high over the goalie's glove. Half a minute later, Turner wrists one high to the other side. It's five-two for us heading into the third.

I have no idea what to expect now but the kids on both teams try to take matters into their own hands. Individually. There's precious little excitement as they all forget it's a team game. Each player tries to run the puck up the middle and virtually no one makes it to either end. Still, I'll be happy if we can hang on for the period. Unfortunately, on the second last shift of the game, a Hawk springs behind us for a breakaway. Tommy has no chance on the hard, high shot. Our lead is two.

I watch the Hawks' coach signal to his goalie. He's about to pull him. Mike and Turner have the final shift. "It'd be great to score a goal here guys," I say, leaning between the two of them once again. "This is a good team. The game's not over. I need you to play your hardest."

The two of them nod and head out for the faceoff. In less than a minute they've made coaching look easy. The puck never leaves the Hawks' end and Mike seals the victory with his fourth. Final score is six-three for us. I can't believe it.

"That was a good game," says Brad, calmly, on the way to the dressing room.

"I thought you said they're the team to beat," says George. "Did they lose their best kid?"

"No. They still have two guys who practice with the Rep team. Believe me, they are good."

In the dressing room, Mike and Turner stand beside each other, peeling equipment off. Both are beaming. "Did you see me go around that guy and one-timer it at the goalie?" says Turner.

"Yeah or when you passed it to me and I nailed it top shelf?" replies Mike.

Their eyes dance, oblivious to the fact there were no one-timers or top-shelf shots in the game they played. They don't even look as the equipment lands on the floor, sometimes in their bag and sometimes not. Turner's mom smiles as she watches the two of them, every now and then reaching down to straighten out the tossed equipment.

Other parents talk in the middle of the dressing room. They too are all smiles, laughing and commending each other on the play of their sons.

Once at home, I take up my natural position, in front of the TV, wine in hand. As usual, my eyes watch the Leafs while my mind replays the Cougars. I can't get over the fact we won by a six-three score. I'm positive they were bigger and faster. "Did they seem faster to you?" I ask my wife, who lies down on the sofa opposite.

Once it's clarified which game I'm referring to, she agrees that from the stands we looked much slower. "But you guys scored when you had the chance. They spent more time in your end, but they couldn't get the puck to the net."

Shoot it up the boards, I think to myself. Simple and effective. No question we were doing it and they weren't. Could it make that much difference? I picture three Hawk forwards skating hard into our end as the puck goes past them on the boards to one of our players, who then takes it down the ice and shoots.

"Defencemen," I shout in our dressing room before the next game, "what did we do last week ten times better than the other team?"

"Shoot it up the boards," yells Braeden.

"That's right. In fact that's the main reason we won. Every time they got in our end, we took the puck off them and shot it up the boards. Just like the best teams do. And forwards, where did we score our goals from? Mike, when you scored last week, where were you?"

"In front of the net."

"That's right. That's where all our goals are coming from. So where should we try to get the puck?"

"In front of the net," yell three forwards in unison.

I make it a pattern before every game. Shoot it up the boards. Pass it out front. Plain and simple. Nothing fancy. Just a couple of things to focus on. It works. Not just one week, or one team, but again and again. We become the best in the league at those two simple tasks. Other teams need three or four rushes to get a shot; we get shots on every rush. No one beats us for almost two months. It's seven games later. For the first time in a while I look at the standings. Our unbeaten streak has put us one win away from first place. I check the schedule to see who we play next. It's the Giants, the team that killed us the last time, with the coaches who laughed at me. *Interesting.*

OUR FIRST BIG GAME

With two months passed, I'm getting to know the boys individually. But it's not the traditional way you get to know someone. Ryan's a perfect example. He has yet to say a word to me but I feel like I know him well. While one of our most skilled players, he's smart enough to listen. He almost always performs a drill the right way, on the first try. In games, he won't back down from anyone. He's small in stature but one of the most tenacious kids you'll see. He skates hard for the entire two-minute shift, and if he can't beat you one way, he'll find another.

Luke, too, has yet to utter a word in my direction and often blushes when I speak to him. But it isn't hard to see his quiet determination. At season's start, his speed was average. But through his face mask, his eyes revealed just how much he wanted to catch the quicker boys. Each week he performed the skating drills as hard as he could. It paid dividends since speed is now an asset. He listens well, but his determination often works against him. He wants to take matters into his own hands, forgetting that using a teammate might make it easier. However, with his strong will to succeed, it's only a matter of time before he figures out teamwork too.

That's how it is. I'm getting to know them through their actions and reactions, rather than words. And for the most part I'm impressed. I don't want to make it out to be more than it is, but really, it's as if you're seeing the human spirit before it's been worn down. Nobody's told these kids what they can't do, so they still believe they can do anything. At practice, they're like sponges, anxious to try whatever's next and prove they can do it. In games, nothing fazes them. We can be down two or three goals, or ahead by a goal—either way they play just as hard.

In my working life, every time you turn around, rules, policies or people tell you why you can't do something, even when doing it makes perfect sense. People even proudly tell you to do the wrong thing, claiming company policy. Seeing the courage these kids have to try anything, and to succeed through effort and determination, is making my sabbatical a very good experience. I never would have dreamed coaching could be so inspirational.

"Your kids are just better skaters," said the Pythons' coach, as he shook my hand after a game in late November. We'd won nine-four and I had to agree with him. The team that had started the season slower than average, was now pretty quick. Every practice followed the same pattern. Three stations on half an ice surface—power skating, stickhandling and shooting. Working the skills was paying off.

The league posts the standings and players stats, but only at Twin Woods, never at IceTime. Further, they're usually a few weeks behind and, for some reason, not entirely accurate. Game sheets are completed for every game so it's tough to know why the posted results don't match the written ones. I haven't said anything to the convenor since, frankly, I'm not sure I want anyone on our team to know how well we're doing.

Playing for first place, however, causes me to reconsider. After all, at the end of the season, we'll be playing games where it's win or go home. This might be a good opportunity to see how the boys react to a *big game* situation. On the other hand, with everything going our way, why tell the boys something that might distract them?

In the end, I compromise. I let the parents know as a by-the-way comment tucked in an e-mail announcing our next three practices. To the kids, I say nothing.

The big game is slated to start at 6:10 P.M. I arrive at five thirty and immediately discover the two opposing coaches also know what's at stake.

"Winner gets first place, huh?" is the first thing the sports fanatic says to me. I notice both he and his partner are wearing black leather jackets with the Giants logo on the chest and *Coach* written on the sleeve. The logo pictures a giant carrying a hockey stick, and taking a big step, as if he's about to crush whatever's in his path. Every time I see it, his boots look bigger. I know the jackets are custom made and cost at least $250. I wonder if they've noticed my new Cougar baseball cap. It was $12.

"I didn't think we were that close to you guys," I answer.

"You have to track it yourself," says the ex-Junior A player. "The standings on the board aren't accurate."

"Really. If I'd known, I would've looked around for an extra practice. We haven't been playing that well lately."

"No. Neither are we. Good luck though."

It's fun kibitzing with other coaches. Before the game, you have to pretend your team is lousy. After the game, you say, "see what I mean" if you lose or, "I can't believe how well we played" if you win. Everyone does it and it never amounts to an advantage, but it feels like you're part of an inside joke.

As the kids arrive, no one's talking about first place. Either the parents didn't tell or no one's reading my e-mails. The players dress quickly and quietly, just like always. For the pre-game talk, I simply go over the game plan, the same one we used last week. Our defence still shoots the puck up the boards but we're now trying to take the next step in Hockey 101. Instead of asking the defence what they're going to do with the puck in our zone, I ask the forwards.

"Shoot it up the boards," answers Will.

"That's right. So if you want to get the puck, where should you be?"

"On the boards."

"Good man. Did everybody hear that?" I repeat where the forwards should be then draw it out for them. I've recently bought a small whiteboard with hockey rink markings. It allows me to show the boys exactly what I'm talking about. I end by reviewing where our goals came from last week, where they've always come from—shots taken in front of the other team's net. Reminding them works.

"Can we go now?" asks Joel, impatiently.

I laugh. It reminds me how hard I used to listen to pre-game talks when I played. "Yeah, why not. You guys know what you're doing."

As the players skate through the warm-up, I pull Mike and Turner over to the bench. "You guys are up first. Sometimes the other team's a little sleepy at the start. If you take off like it's a race, you might get a goal. Think you can do it?"

Mike nods.

"Sure coach," echoes Turner.

The puck drops. Mike tips it between the other centre's legs and takes off. The two defencemen immediately converge on him. He passes to Turner, zooming down the right side. As Turner crosses the faceoff circle, he shoots but misses the net. Their defenceman quickly retrieves the puck and tries to clear, but Mike intercepts it on the boards. He takes it straight to the net, dekes the other defenceman and shoots high on the stick side. Half a minute in, we're up one-nothing.

The early parts of games are played on freshly flooded ice, an advantage to fast skaters. Today, we're proving we've become just that, since as the puck glides over the slick surface, we're winning the races.

Midway through the first, Braeden banks a clearing pass off the boards in the neutral zone. Travis, a left-handed shot, takes off down the right side. Their defence tries to angle him off but he's too quick. The instant he's past them, he turns toward the net. His wrist shot is high and hard. The goalie doesn't move. It's two-nothing.

The benches are right beside each other, with only a small Plexiglas partition. You can hear what the opposing coaches are saying to their players if you want. I can't resist. This time, the coaches are bewildered. They're not saying much and what they do say is of the stock variety. Things like "Come on, guys, try harder" or "how can you let that happen to you."

Their goalie is one of the bigger kids on the ice. He doesn't appear fast but his size helps him stop most of our shots. Tommy, on the other hand, isn't often tested. As he skates by between periods, I yell "Way to go Tommy" and try to think of something that might help him stay focused. I turn to our defencemen. "From now on, at the start of every shift, I want you to tap Tommy on the pads. He's not getting many shots now but we'll need him later on, okay?" The boys calmly nod, and then look back toward the ice. We are definitely a quiet team.

The second period is similar to the first except we aren't able to score. The Giants are rushing, but our defence is equal to the task. They usually shut them down at our blue line and quickly shoot the puck back up the ice, always off the boards. Our forwards are passing and we're getting shots, but the big kid stops them all.

Early in the third, the Giants finally break through. One of their forwards intercepts our clearing pass and banks it off the boards, around our defence. No one can catch him and his shot eludes Tommy. We've outplayed them all game but now, with less than a period to go, our lead is down to one.

Their bench erupts and the coaches try to seize the momentum, with lots of "See, that's how you do it" and "we can win this boys."

Next up are Mike and Turner. I lean between the two of them. "We need a good shift. If one of you gets the puck, take it wide, near the boards. When the defence follow you, pass it straight back into the middle. Okay? Work together."

The boys nod and hustle out. Once again, they take off like shots when the puck hits the ice. Neither takes it wide but they don't need to. They're simply beating the other players. I leave them out for a minute and a half. The other coaches silently watch as Mike and Turner buzz through and around players, beating them to the puck or simply taking it away from them. They take six shots on goal. One hits the right post dead-on; another caroms off the left. None go in.

"That was a great shift guys," I say as they return to the bench, emphasizing *great*. "Might've been your best all year."

"But we didn't score," replies Mike.

"Doesn't matter. You guys were all over them. It was perfect."

The shift accomplishes exactly what I'd hoped for. It lifts our team and reminds the Giants who's winning this game. Travis' line takes to the ice and keeps up the pressure. Next out is Justin's line. He's been playing well but hasn't scored as often as I thought he'd might. Justin wins the faceoff in their zone and passes the puck straight to Luke on the wing. Luke shoots. The goalie kicks it right back to Justin who makes no mistake, flipping it high into the mesh. We're up by two goals again.

The Giants' coaches are upset. One even throws a towel. But

neither criticizes any player. Instead they calmly tell their boys they're being outskated and outworked.

It's true. And it continues. The play is seldom inside our blue line for the balance of the game. As if putting an exclamation point on it, Mike takes a pass from Justin on a line change, and wings it high into the glove side. The final score is four-one for us.

The Giants' coaches are good sports and quickly shake my hand, telling me how well our team played. I don't laugh and the kids are equally calm and sportsmanlike as they file off the ice. Once inside our dressing room, I give the boys the good news.

"Great game guys. Three cheers—Hip, hip . . ."

"Hooray," they shout.

"Come on, you can do better than that. We won! Hip, hip . . ."

"Hooray," they shout louder.

"Now come on. I want to hear your loudest. We're in first place! Hip, hip . . ."

Instantly, several eyes widen. As it turns out, most didn't know, and the last "Hooray" is nowhere near as loud as the second. Turner rushes up to me.

"We're in first place, Coach?" he asks, anticipation etched on his wide-eyed face.

"That's right. And just to make sure everyone knows," I add, raising my voice over the din, "the winner of that game got first place and we won."

Some kids laugh, others scream. Two even hug each other. The parents arrive. It turns out some don't read their e-mail, since they also ask for confirmation. A couple of parents shake my hand and congratulate me. Around the room forty faces smile and laugh.

The good feelings last through the weekend and into the next week. We have a six o'clock practice Wednesday morning, which means waking up at quarter after five. Almost the entire team shows up. By contrast, the team we share the ice with, has but four players. We agree to practice together and end with a kids-versus-dads scrimmage.

On the way out of the arena, I glance at the bulletin board to see if they've updated the standings. They haven't but underneath they've posted the leading scorers. Mike's number one and Turner's number two. No one else is close.

When we get home, I can't resist going through the game sheets. I'd realized Mike was scoring but assumed others would be too. The notion he'd be leading the league hadn't occurred to me. The game sheets confirm the impact he's had on our team. In quite a few games Mike's outscored the other team all on his own. It's happened in so many games that I can't resist making a list. After all, I'm not just his coach—I'm his father, and pride is definitely taking hold.

The truth is startling. We're in first place, but if you take away the goals Mike's scored or assisted on, we're seventh—second last. I have to smile. I wanted Mike to do well and he has. First in scoring. First place team. What a season!

A few hours later, though, I'm bugged. I'm happy for Mike, but why aren't more of the others players scoring? Are we really a one-line team? For the last couple of weeks parents have been telling me how well I'm doing. Now I wonder. A team that depends on one line or even one player is definitely not the sign of a good coach. We are in first place and I do think we're on the right track, but if I'm really a good coach, we need everybody going. The only problem is, I have no idea what more I can do.

PLAYING LIKE THE PROS

Every kid watches and likes to pretend they're on *Hockey Night in Canada*. In my day, we were Keon, Mahovlich or Horton. Today, they're Kariya, Forsberg and Sakic. I want to capitalize on that professional fantasy in the Cougar experience.

I start by naming drills after pro players. Our Sundin drill is a stop/start exercise that Mats used to come back from injury—great for teaching kids to stop on both sides. The Kariya drill is an edgework move I saw Paul do before a game—it improves balance by forcing you to turn on your inside foot. Both are challenging drills, but the kids complete them.

The nearest NHL team to us is one of the most storied—the Toronto Maple Leafs. I've followed them since the age of five. I literally cried when they lost the Stanley Cup final to Montreal in 1965. In 1967, when they won the Cup, I wrote the names of my favourite players around the boards of my tabletop hockey set. In my arena, their numbers were retired.

Ticket prices are such that taking the team to a game is out of the question, but the Leafs hold several events for minor hockey players. Surfing through their Web site, I find one that fits perfectly.

I sign up our team to watch a game day skate at the Air Canada Centre. Amazingly, it's free.

We arrive early Saturday morning. The arena staff escorts us, en masse, to the Gold Section, only fifty feet from the ice. Other kids and parents file in—about thirty teams in total. We've just taken our seats when the Leafs emerge from the dressing room. Although the practice jerseys are blank, the kids call out the names the instant they step on the ice. Mats Sundin, Curtis Joseph and Tie Domi draw the biggest applause, but on this day, everyone gets recognized.

I'm curious to see what drills the Leafs run, recording them on a piece of paper I've brought. I figure there has to be one or two we can use for our practices. It turns out even better. Although they have their own way of running them, every drill the Leafs do is, at heart, one that we've already done in practice. I take great pride in pointing out to the kids that the two-on-ones, one-on-ones and the three-on-nones they're watching, are the same ones they've done back home. The boys don't care. They're mesmerized, watching their heroes dart around the ice. The skating is faster and the shots harder than any they've seen before. We're so close, you can hear the players on the ice, particularly when they tease or laugh at each other. It's great.

We're allowed to stay for the visiting team's skate. Today, it's the Pittsburgh Penguins. As they take the ice, in the middle of the pack, out comes Mario Lemieux, smiling broadly and waving to the crowd. For their first drill, the Penguins skate slowly around the ice. A coach appears. He blows the whistle and the players take off, skating hard. Nearly every kid in the arena turns to his buddy saying, "Hey, we do that."

I've heard that visiting teams like to practice in front of the kids, and everything the Penguins do is a traditional minor hockey drill. It occurs to me one of the players might've suggested it to connect with the kids. The way Mario's smiling and carrying on makes me think it was him. Regardless, it's a great touch and will make my job easier when we get back to the practice rink.

As we file out, fathers and sons chat about plays they saw or how certain players look in person. It's hard to tell who enjoyed it more—the boys or the dads.

Our finances won't allow us to see an NHL game, but the nearby Ontario Junior A Mississauga IceDogs offer a five-dollar discount on the price of group tickets. Although not currently doing particularly well themselves, in a few weeks they play one of the league leaders. I arrange to get tickets.

Since this is the first time most have seen either team, I give the boys a list of names to watch for. The names do well. Every one on my list scores, and two of them finish with hat tricks. Even better, we're seated behind the net and have a perfect view of each team setting up its breakout and attack plays. It's lost on the kids but I enjoy it.

Watching the Cougar games as a coach has changed the way I'm seeing all games. Every Saturday night, I still stretch out in the same chair, but now I'm looking for things I didn't notice before. I'll watch what the players without the puck do, or follow one player for an entire shift. I try to spot patterns in the way a team attacks or defends. Once you start, you see different approaches. The Leafs like to break out against the grain. They set up to go one way, and then reverse direction. It works, but to my eyes, not as often as the simpler ways other teams use. It's amazing how many times I see a pro team break out of their zone in the same way the Cougars do—a pass up the boards to a winger.

One Saturday night, I watch the referee call a penalty, and suddenly remember I still haven't taught the boys any of hockey's rules. I did that for all of my soccer teams and, frankly, was something I felt good about. In hockey, I have been chastising players who commit fouls in practice but still, I want the kids to know there's a rule book where everything's written down in black and white.

Unfortunately, it's been a tough start. It took me a month to get my hands on the actual rule book. The league doesn't give us one, it isn't in my coach's manual and I couldn't find a copy in the library or on the Internet. Later I discovered our regional association provides them by mail for a nominal fee. Since it arrived, I've been through it but I've yet to decide which rule to start with. Now seems like a good time to decide.

As in other sports, reading the written rule proves painful but ultimately educational. It's the little things you notice. Reading the offside rule, for instance, indicates whether the puck has to cross the entire blue line or just touch it before the attacking team must retreat out of the zone. Glancing through the book, I make notes. I'm looking for a rule the kids will think they know, but in truth, don't. Reading over the slashing rule convinces me it's a perfect place to start.

I smile as I picture exactly how I'll teach the boys. First, I'll ask for a volunteer, take a stick and pretend to slash him across the leg. Then I'll ask if it's a penalty. No doubt everyone will shout yes. Then I'll slash the volunteer's stick, up high, near his hands. This time when I ask, the room will go quiet. One might say yes, another no. I'll force them to take a side by asking for a show of hands. I know what will happen. Most will say it's not a penalty, which will be great, because it is. That's the best way for kids to remember. Take a guess and find out they're wrong.

But it won't stop there. Once they know slashing the shaft of the stick is a penalty, I'll ask about slashing the blade of the stick, reminding them the volunteer is carrying the puck. Once again, they'll be unsure and have to guess. Hopefully they'll guess wrong and I can state categorically it's okay to hit the blade of another player's stick when he's carrying the puck.

Lastly, I'll swing my stick through the air, missing the volunteer entirely, and ask for a final vote. All will say it is definitely not a penalty. Then I'll pull out the rule book and read aloud: "A player who swings his stick at an opponent and makes no contact shall still be guilty of slashing." From that day forward, most of the team will have the slashing rule down cold. Then I'll do the same with hooking, tripping, offsides. By the end of the season, they'll have a good understanding of hockey's rules.

I return to the game on TV as the puck is dumped into the Leafs' zone. Players fight for it in the corner. I look in front of the net. Leaf defenceman, Brian McCabe, cross-checks his opponent across the shoulder blades. Once, twice, three times, chasing his opponent behind the net. When the forward regains the puck, Thomas Kaberle is on him. First, he slashes his leg, then the shaft of the stick. The player passes off, but the Leafs intercept and chip it over the blue line. Neither referee has blown his whistle or raised his hand.

Mats Sundin picks up the puck and streaks down the right boards. A defender tries to angle in on him, but he's a stride behind. So he reaches ahead and hooks his stick around Sundin's hips, pulling himself to where he can hook the elbow. Sundin uses his hand to take the defending player's stick off him. But he has to pass, and one-hands it toward the front of the net. Gary Roberts arrives as the puck does, but another defender has grabbed his arms and stick so tightly, Roberts can't move. The puck slides into the corner.

"Whoa, did you see that?" asks Joe, lying on the couch.

I listen for Mike's reply, wondering how many infractions he noticed.

"Yeah," says Mike, "all he had to do was tip it."

Wow—they didn't notice any. Is that how they think hockey is played? Slashes, cross-checks, hooks; in front of your own net, anything goes. I must admit, that's what they see every week. I wonder how many players on our team are watching this very game. Or how many on the team we'll be playing. It could easily be all of them. In fact, the guy who'll be refereeing our game is probably watching too. We're all seeing the way hockey is played, what's called and what's not.

The next morning at breakfast, I can't resist pursuing it a little further. "Do you think there's much slashing in the NHL?" I ask.

"Yeah," replies Mike, in a tone that suggests it's a pretty stupid question—obviously there's lots of slashing in the NHL.

"Is that okay?"

"No, but they all do it."

"Then why do they have a slashing rule?"

Mike shrugs.

"I don't think it's okay," interjects Joe. "Because then kids do it. They see a guy in the NHL slash so they do it too."

I ask if there's much slashing in their leagues. Predictably, they both claim there is. But they don't think they've ever slashed anyone. When I ask if they'd ever turn and slash someone back if they knew the ref wasn't looking, Joe says it depends on how much it hurt. Mike claims he wouldn't do it if he got slashed, but he might if a teammate did. When I ask if that's playing by the rules, their answers surprise me. Although they initially say it's not, after thinking it over, they come to the conclusion there aren't any rules in hockey.

"Like, there are rules," explains Joe, accenting are, "but because they don't call them, really there aren't any."

"Yeah," agrees Mike, in a tone that suggests he's surprised to actually agree with his brother.

I'd planned to bring the rule book to practice this week. Suddenly it doesn't seem like such a great idea. There's a clear pattern emerging in our games. The refs call one rule, and only one rule—offside. Even then, they'd miss several if it weren't for a parent or coach yelling. Players' legs and ankles get slashed routinely without any call. A punch to Ryan's head still didn't draw a penalty. In the early season I figured it was because the ref just missed it. But after I started watching where they positioned themselves and what they were looking at, I could see their eyes were focused squarely on the infraction. But they would never call it. Whenever I took it up with them, the stock reply was "Really? I didn't see it," or "They're just kids, they can't hurt anyone." A kid slashing a kid is no different than an adult slashing an adult. Further, the kids grow into men believing the infractions are perfectly legal.

Part of me says if I don't teach the rules, I'm contributing to the problem. But at the same time, I can't escape the reality of the situation. They're not making the calls in our league, nor are they making them in the NHL. What is the point of teaching rules that aren't followed? Just so a bunch of kids can tell me what's being missed?

No. I won't teach them to cheat but I won't handicap them with the rules that aren't called. I'll make sure they understand offside, icing, where to stand on face-offs. But help kids understand slashing, interference? Not a chance. They can learn those rules the same way every other kid does. By watching the non-calls in the NHL and in our league. I'll be honest if they ask, but there's no way I'm going to stand up and pretend we're playing by the rules in the rule book. We're not. And neither are the pros.

EVERYONE'S FORWARD

At the start of the season I warned the parents we'd begin by rotating positions, then we'd decide where each boy was best suited to play, and leave him there. The kids learn far more about hockey and teamwork when they stay in the same spot week after week. Moreover, the team plays better. It was perfectly logical and in everyone's best interest. I even had a few parents write to me expressing their approval. The only problem was making sure each kid felt good about their assigned role.

At first I thought giving everyone a turn at centre, and a little time at every position, would minimize any bad feelings if a boy didn't get the position he wanted. Then I came up with an even better idea.

"Which position is the most important on a hockey team?" I asked to start a pre-game speech.

"Forward," yelled a couple, straight off. But after I asked why Paul Kariya and Teemu Selanne—two of the best forwards the game has seen—couldn't take their team to the playoffs, the boys could see it wasn't forward.

"Goalie," said Tommy. A few others quickly agreed. But when I pointed out Dominik Hasek has been the best goalie in the NHL for six years but couldn't bring the Buffalo Sabres a Stanley Cup, they could see it wasn't goalie.

"Defence?" asked Simon.

"Two of the NHL's best defencemen, Chris Pronger and Al MacInnis, play on one team. But that team hasn't been close to winning a Cup."

The room was silent. It was clear they understood. Or so I thought.

"I know," said Braeden, with an air of finality. "The coach is the most important."

Brad, George and I chuckled.

"No. A coach can't score any goals or even stop any. It has to be a player. So which position's the most important?"

"They all are," answered Travis.

"That's right. It doesn't matter what position you play. We need every player to try his hardest. If we're going to win, we need good defence, a good goalie and good forwards. It doesn't matter where you play. Everyone's important."

By November, the stage was set. I froze the lines and waited. Amazingly, it seemed to work. I overheard Simon, a boy who'd only ever played forward, telling his linemates he liked defence. Justin was proud to be centre. And Turner was ecstatic playing alongside Mike week in and week out. To my eyes at least, the kids were happy, the lineup looked good, and we were winning. But I forgot to give the speech to the parents.

"T.J.," starts Kevin's mother, on the phone one Monday morning, "I thought you'd better know. Kevin was crying after our last game." Kevin's mom has been a big help to the team. She made loot bags for our trip to the Air Canada Centre and told me she'd do anything to help, provided she didn't have to go to any meetings. She sounded like someone I could relate to.

"You're kidding. I didn't see anything. Did he get hurt?"

"No. It's the defence. He hates playing defence. He's always played forward, his brothers play forward. That's what he wants. He told me he doesn't want to play hockey any more. I don't know what to do."

Kevin is a quiet kid that, every now and then, likes to clown around. He's never struck me as someone who cared that much about hockey, much less what position he played. "We had him on forward but he was hanging back all the time so I thought . . ."

"I know. And we've told him, Kevin, you got to get in there. It's something he really needs to work on."

"Yeah, but normally, kids who hang back, do it because they like to see the play evolve. Those are the kids who make the best defencemen. That's usually where they're happiest."

"Well, not Kevin. He says . . ."

The conversation continues for a full thirty-five minutes. The content stays the same. There will be no joy in Kevin's world until he gets to play forward. I'm glad the mom is on the team but I don't like being told how to coach. I continue to resist, rephrasing my argument as many different ways as I can, all to no avail. In the end, a compromise is reached. Kevin will continue on defence for a "few weeks" and I'll reconsider at that time.

"Oh, Kevin will be so happy," exclaims his mother. "And you don't need to worry. The next time he's on forward, we'll make sure he doesn't hang back." It occurs to me the mother would make a great forward.

But it's not just the position that irks some parents, it's the linemates.

"That number seven refuses to pass," Ryan's mom confronts me, as I'm about to leave the dressing room for practice. "You know passing is a skill that can be taught." This is the first time I've heard from her. Ryan's dad dresses him and they're usually first in the dressing room. We've had many conversations and I thought we were getting along.

"Uh, yes," I reply, taken aback. "I don't know if you've seen any of our practices but, we actually work on passing every week. That's why we do the drills we're doing."

"Well it doesn't seem to be working, does it? When his linemates are open he should pass. Have you spoken to him?"

Number seven is Travis. His father, Dave, played the game for over thirty years and continues to be a big help at practice. "I know his dad tries to get him to see the ice better and to look for linemates."

"Oh. So the father recognizes there's a problem."

Ryan's mom is unaware that "the father" has come back in the dressing room and is standing right behind her. From the look on his face, I can see Dave's heard most of what she's said.

"Yeah . . . I guess." The few seconds it takes me to figure out what to say, feel more like a long, uncomfortable hour. "It's tough for the good players to pass. They know they can beat most of their opponents so, actually, the better you are, the harder it is to figure out when to pass." It's the truth. One on one, Travis can beat ninety percent of the players in this league. So from his perspective, it's tough to know when, or why, to pass.

Dave quickly ducks out of the dressing room. Ryan's mom is still staring into my eyes.

"Well, it's not much fun playing with someone who never passes. We tell Ryan he can still go for the rebounds but it would be much better to have teammates who pass."

I can't remember Travis missing any obvious passing opportunities but I do recall Ryan banging his stick on the ice a couple of times during games. Ryan is also a good player, but you can't expect someone to pass the puck just because you want it.

"I wouldn't worry," I say, as reassuringly as I can, "today we're doing one-on-ones followed by two-on-ones. The kids see for themselves how much easier it is to get by someone when you pass."

"Well, I hope it works," she replies, turning to leave, "because they'll never win if they don't learn to pass."

But we are winning, I think to myself. Or at least we had been.

Our first game as league leaders is a solid effort, but proves that all unbeaten streaks must come to an end. We fall to the Huskies four-three. Fortunately, the Giants also lose so we remain in first place. Unfortunately, at least from the coach's perspective, the Mike–Will–Turner line scores all our goals.

The following week, we resume our winning ways, beating the Sharks four-one. Even better, all three lines contribute. Our next victims are the Falcons. It's my birthday and the boys give me a great present. We score on our first shift and never look back in a seven-one romp.

Heading into Christmas, we're alone in first and clearly on a roll. I remember the day I dreaded having signed us up for a Select tournament over the holidays. Now I can't wait. As I watch the Leafs in their last pre-holiday match, I dream of Cougars becoming the first house league team to win a tournament for all-stars.

A HOCKEY EDUCATION

Despite my Canadian citizenship, I knew at the start of the season that to be a good coach I needed to acquire a hockey education beyond what my birthright had given me. The few days off before our Christmas tournament gave me a chance to reflect on what I'd done and what I'd learned. The education came in two ways: through my own efforts, and through the hockey authorities.

For my part, I approached the task the same way I had in my soccer days. I went to the library and took out every book and video I could find on skating, coaching and teaching hockey. It worked. I found some great resources that broke the hockey skills down into manageable pieces, whether it was skating, shooting or stickhandling. It was then easy to create drills appropriate for eight-year-olds. I had two rules: the drills had to be simple and they had to recreate a game situation.

So week after week we practiced things that could easily be explained and demonstrated. Race to the puck, pick it up and bring it back; stickhandle through a zigzag pylon course with your head up; or, stand at the hash marks and take fifteen shots on goal. Easy. Simple. Effective.

Team situations were no different; we practiced one-on-ones, two-on-ones, three-on-twos. Anything that might crop up in a game and would make the complex world of five-on-five hockey, easier for a youngster to understand.

The second part of my hockey education—the official curriculum for rookies like me—was much more difficult, and surprisingly, of limited value on the ice.

It started early in the season, with a one-night seminar provided for first-time coaches by our league. The instructor led us through a thick handout that covered the various rule books (our town's, the region's and Hockey Canada's), an overview of the administrative duties associated with running a hockey team, game day tasks, sample budgets, player evaluations, parent letters, medical information sheets and a sample practice plan. They also included a fifty-page Hockey Canada booklet entitled *Getting Started in Hockey*. The handouts contained some useful information—practical things like who to call for printing the names on jerseys—but I was surprised how little space was devoted to the actual teaching of hockey. Over half of the sample drills were full-ice—not much use for the half-ice practices we get. Nowhere did I find any suggestions for breaking the ice up into stations, the way we've done it.

"You guys won't like this," warned the head official of house league at the introductory meeting, "but starting this year, every head coach needs to be *Speak Out* certified."

He was referring to a new program put in place as a reaction to the child abuse stories that have cropped up recently in minor hockey. Each member of the coaching staff must complete a police check (at a cost of fifteen dollars each), and the head coach must attend a three-hour seminar on player abuse. The session started with a video depicting a coach shouting criticism at his players. I didn't mention it, but I'd seen worse. We then broke into small groups to discuss the video and how badly the coach acted. Ironically, one of the most vocal people in the room was a fellow with a reputation for being a verbally abusive coach. Joe's team shared the ice with him one memorable Sunday last year. He berated his players so loudly at one end of the rink, Joe's team couldn't hear their own coach at the other end. Strangely enough, his boys had won their game—he was upset they'd allowed so many goals. On this day, he was talking about the need to remain cool, calm and above all, positive when dealing with kids.

There is a need for coaches to talk about issues like these but clearly, it's easy to be rational with a group of adults in a boardroom, and not as easy when you're behind the bench, watching players and referees make mistakes. I'm later told that Graham James—the infamous coach who sexually abused his players—would have passed a police check and would probably have enjoyed the *Speak Out* video.

Early in September, I registered for the course to get my coaching licence. When I arrived home, I noticed the clinic was being held at the league's office. I'd heard it was supposed to be at an arena so I called back to double-check. They confirmed.

"So it's eight thirty at the hockey office, then we go to a rink in the afternoon?" I asked.

"That's right," she replied, "but you don't need to be here till nine o'clock. Registration is from eight thirty to nine, but it only takes a minute."

Be there for 9 A.M., I wrote on my calendar, next to the phone.

On the appointed day, almost two months later, I arrived, ten minutes early, just to be safe. The boardroom door was closed and another coach was arguing outside the room with the head of House League.

"Sorry but it's not my rule," said the head official, "if you're even five minutes late, they won't let you in."

"But the sheet said nine o'clock."

"No it didn't. Everything in writing said eight thirty. You'll have to go to a clinic somewhere else."

Then it was my turn to confront the man and explain what I was told. I was just as successful getting into the course. Apparently six different coaches thought it started at nine and all six were turned away. I later found out the Giants' coaches were also told nine but they called the night before to double-check, and were then informed about the time change.

It wasn't a trivial matter. To begin with, the kids can't play in a tournament unless their coach is licensed. We'd already paid six hundred dollars for our tournament fee. Secondly, it's November and there aren't many more clinics before the Christmas season. When I called around for openings, there weren't any. They told me the only way my team could play was to show up at clinics that were full, and hope somebody who registered didn't come.

The coaching licence I wanted is called Level One and is good for all age groups. It's a two-day course and costs one hundred dollars. Unfortunately, when I showed up at the next clinic (an eight o'clock start), everyone who registered arrived on time.

A less desirable alternative is the Canadian Hockey Initiation Program, or CHIP licence. It's a one-day course that costs fifty dollars, but is only good for coaching younger kids. Still, it would solve my short-term problem, so I showed up at one of those clinics a half hour away. At eight o'clock, I was given the news—one individual didn't show. I was in.

The fellow conducting the course had coached for over thirty years. The material in the binder we're given didn't look too useful, but the session leader was soon providing us with anecdotes from his coaching days and any tip he could think of (for example, how to teach kids to stop on their skates). Once everyone realized he had some useful pointers, the binders closed and we turned the day into a coaching question and answer session. Ironically, one suggestion he emphasized as a "must do" was to split the ice into stations—one for skating, shooting and stickhandling. I had to smile as he explained the rationale. Apparently the station idea was only new to me, and I didn't invent it. Older coaches have used it for years.

The day ended at a local rink, where we taught a few volunteer five-year-olds how to skate, shoot or stickhandle. When I was handed the licence at the end of the day, I was relieved.

But it wasn't just the art and administration of coaching I needed to learn, it was also the structure of hockey. And to be clear, hockey is most definitely structured.

"Do you have a list of tournaments we could enter?" I remember asking innocently in September.

At the time, I thought entering a kids' team in a hockey tournament would be easy and simple—choose a tournament, register the team. But there was nothing simple or easy about it.

First, a master list of tournaments does not exist. I found this out by accident. The Ontario Minor Hockey Association (OMHA) governs our town's hockey program. For some silly reason, I thought this was the association that governs minor hockey in Ontario. It isn't. Contrary to its name, it has jurisdiction over only a small part of the province, and none of the largest cities. So the tournament listing on its Web site was only a portion of the tourneys being played in Ontario.

After a few days surfing the Internet and asking other coaches, I learned that Ontario hockey is split into six "regional" associations. I use the term regional loosely because they aren't based on geographical boundaries. Looking at which towns belong to which regions, it appears that for at least a few towns, adult politics have played more of a role in determining their affiliation, than what's in the best interest of kids. Some towns have teams in two regions, thus diluting their talent. In other cases, a town belongs to a different region than its neighbouring towns. Therefore, its Rep teams have to drive much further to play hockey.

I had neither the time nor the inclination to find out why there were three regions operating within twenty miles of my house, but there are. Each with its own tournament lists. Adding insult to injury, there were even tournaments I knew were taking place, that didn't appear on any list.

I also thought choosing the age level would be straightforward. It wasn't. Our boys are eight years old—Minor Novice in hockey-speak. Unfortunately, several towns group eight- and nine-year-olds together, calling it Novice. Since many tournaments can't attract enough Minor Novice teams, they only run a Novice division. So I had to decide whether to play only against boys the same age, or whether we could play against teams a year older.

I also had to determine which classification our team fell into. Each tournament classes itself at a certain level to ensure the teams playing each other are relatively balanced and the games are competitive. I looked for Gold House League. It wasn't there—on any list, in any region. A total of nineteen different ways were used for classifying an eight-year-old boys' hockey team, from AAA to DD to AE and more, but Gold House League wasn't one of them.

In the end, it seemed the best alternatives were either Minor Novice Select (boys our age who've been selected the best in their league) or Novice House League (boys that might be a year older but could be anywhere from first to worst in their league). I like to challenge kids so I chose Minor Novice Select and found one operated by a well-established hockey association in Toronto. All I had to do was register the team. Easy enough, or at least, so I thought.

To be registered, there are certain requirements. The team must have a licensed coach and a licensed trainer. Brad has his trainer's licence and after the aforementioned running around, I had my coach's, but it turned out Brad's licence was issued in another region (ten miles away). It has to be registered in our region. To accomplish this, he didn't have to take a test or anything, just pay a fee (twenty dollars).

Next, for what I'm told are "insurance reasons," to take our team out of town, we had to apply for a travel permit. Because the tournament was out of region, we also had to pay a fee of twenty dollars. The permit itself was a very simple one-page document. We faxed it to the region one morning, and received the signed fax back that afternoon.

Lastly, all our players and parents had to sign individual registration cards and all coaches had to sign team official cards, as well as the team registration form. The entire package had to be submitted to both the league and region for approval. The devil's advocate in me wondered what an individual in another town would do to "approve" a list of names, addresses and birthdates for people he didn't know, but rather than ask, I dutifully completed every form exactly as instructed.

We received the entire package of approved forms, cards and licences, with requisite signatures in place, the week before Christmas. At long last the eight-year-olds could play hockey.

CHRISTMAS MORNINGS IN TORONTO

It isn't the "administrivia" occupying my thoughts as I lie wide awake in bed, at two in the morning, the night before our first game in the Big City Select Christmas Tournament. My worries are more hockey-related. Have I overestimated the boys in signing them up for a Select tournament? The team we play tomorrow, the host team, features their league's all-star players. There's no way we'd beat an all-star team from our league. This could be a disaster.

Furthermore, our schedule is brutal—all early morning games. We won't be able to hold a team lunch unless we make it to the playoff round. To do so, we'll have to finish in the top half of the twelve teams entered. Remembering makes me feel better. We may not win this but we should be in the top half.

At three o'clock, I'm still awake. My mind has moved on to Murphy's Law–type issues. What if a snowstorm blows in overnight and half our team arrives late? Our opponents live in Toronto and they'll be on time. Our game starts at seven o'clock and we have to be there an hour early to sign in. What if the alarm sounds, I turn it off and go back to sleep? I check to make sure the alarm is on. It is. And what about all that stupid paperwork? What if we arrive and discover we can't play because I didn't fill out some form I've never heard of? It happened to at least one coach I know. His entire team had to turn around and make the two-hour drive back home. I sent an e-mail to the tournament organizer a week ago telling him what papers I'd be bringing and asking if I needed anything else. He didn't respond. I make a mental note to bring a copy of that e-mail.

I'm up before the five o'clock alarm and sure enough, a light dusting of snow has fallen overnight. Mike wakes easily, which is unusual for him. He says he had a good sleep but I doubt it. The highway is empty. The only other time I remember seeing a Toronto freeway so clear was twenty years ago when I was coming home at three thirty in the morning. It makes me think only a fool would get up this early on his Christmas holidays to play hockey.

We're at the arena by quarter to six but the parking lot is empty and the lights in the reception area are dim. I can see the tournament banner hanging so I know we're in the right spot. But not even the arena personnel have arrived. Mike and I head back to an all night doughnut shop we passed on the way in.

At quarter after six we're back at the arena and this time, it's open. Players have started to arrive. By six thirty, it's abuzz with parents, kids, tournament organizers and innocent bystanders milling about. I exchange my car keys for a dressing room key, and an organizer asks me to bring the boys out to sign a team list. When Mike signs, I gaze over the other so-called signatures—virtually all of them are first names only, printed. This group of athletes hasn't learned to write cursively.

The team we're playing has the full set of all-star accoutrements. All players wear the same green leather jacket, with their numbers stitched on the sleeve. Their equipment bags are also colour and number coordinated. Some of the boys have green toques with the team logo on the front. One of the boy's parents is standing by the wall, near the entrance to our dressing room.

"Hi," I say as our eyes meet, "Are you with the Axemen?"

The man is friendly and fills me in on his son's team. The Axemen represent the best players from two all-star squads for their league. They play two games and practice at least twice every week—one for each of their house league and select teams. When you add tournaments, exhibition games and extra practices, he's taking his son to an arena almost every day. As for how they're doing in league play, he claims "middle of the pack."

As the boys get dressed, I wander out to the ice surface. I look forward to visiting arenas I've never been in. Each one has its own unique feel and smells. I like to imagine the games they've hosted and conflicts that have taken place. Maybe it says more about me than I should admit, but when I was in Rome, I thought the Colosseum looked like a hockey rink. When I learned what went on in that arena, it helped me understand why the parent spectators get so excited in ours. They watch their kids, dressed like gladiators, playing a dangerous game in an enclosed area; there's nothing the parents can do to help them.

This arena is empty. The ice is clear. The building looks like a Mennonite bank barn, but there's nothing rustic about it. Wooden planks the colour of oak flooring line the ceiling. They look new. The concrete walls and floors are painted grey and are so clean they almost shine. The stands behind the player's benches are green, the home team's colour. I don't hate it but you get the sense the home players arrive in BMWs.

As I head back to the dressing room, a freshly-shaven man in a green jacket stops me. He hands me a puck and tells me I have to pick the Player of the Game for the other team. I glance down at the puck. It's brand new except one side has the green tournament logo, with the words *Player of the Game 2001* written around it.

"Let's ask Dave to do it," offers Brad. "He'll be in the stands. He can pick the best one."

The dressing room is a little noisier than usual as the kids compare what they got for Christmas. I've decided my pre-game talk will be the same as always, except I'll take a few minutes to remind the boys it doesn't matter whether it's House League, Select or the NHL—whoever puts the puck in front of the other team's net most often, will probably win the game.

The kids don't even pause as they head out into the arena and step onto the ice. No looking around, or glancing into the stands, just the same old skating in a circle to warm up.

"You can tell they're Select," says Brad as we watch the other team. "There's no duds on that team."

Mike, Turner and Will are due to take the opening faceoff. The play starts at a fast pace. The all-stars skate and handle the puck well, but so do we. They break in and get a shot, we clear, break in and get a shot of our own. It's shaping up to be an end-to-end game. They shift, we shift; they headman, we headman. Just as I'm starting to think we really can play with these guys, the puck gets behind our defence. One of their fastest forwards beats everyone to the puck and has a breakaway. He puts it high to make it one-nothing.

"It's okay boys," I say, "We'll get it back. Let's go."

But on the very next shift, they score again on a breakaway. It's early and we're down by two. Still, our boys hang in and it's not even another minute before we have a breakaway of our own. Mike takes it all the way from centre ice and shoots. He hits the post. Two minutes later, Justin streaks behind their defence for another breakaway.

"Okay, here we go," I say to the bench. "This is it."

Justin's shot misses the net and the score stays the same. The Axemen continue to get chances but Tommy's focused and playing well. Early in the second, Mike gets yet another breakaway. This time he dekes, a sure fire goal if ever there was one. Not this time. The goalie's fooled, but for the first time this season, Mike's finish goes wide.

"The puck slid off my stick," he says when he returns to the bench.

"It's okay. We're getting our chances. They can't hold us off forever." But they do. The missed chances are the story of the game. We have as many quality shots, but no goals. All we can hit are posts, crossbars and the boards behind the net. Late in the third, Travis even puts one over the net—everything but mesh.

The all-stars close out the game with three goals to hand us our worst defeat of the season: six-nothing. It wasn't a lopsided game, but it's hard to feel positive with the scoreboard showing what it does. The other coaches picked our goalie as MVP. Tommy did have a good game—the scoring chances were even but their finishes were better. Still, with the score what it is, choosing the goalie strikes me as a bit cheeky. We identified a couple of their players as standouts. The coaches thank us and say they'll give it to the boy who scored the most goals.

On the way to the dressing room, Ryan's dad stops me. "Ryan got one shift the whole second period," he says, his eyes blazing. He flashes his index finger in front of me to emphasize the point. "One shift. That's crazy."

"Uh, really?" I say, trying to be calm. "I didn't know."

"You guys have to move the lines faster. It's ridiculous."

He turns and heads back to the rink. I know he's disappointed. He was looking forward to this tournament as much as I was; like me, he thought we'd have a chance. A six-nothing whipping is not the expected start.

As I enter the dressing room, the kids are changing quickly. "Okay guys, you have to remember, that team gets two games and two practices every week. We did alright. The game was a lot closer than the score, that's for sure. Let's have our three cheers."

After the muted cheers, the room clears in little more than five minutes. Ryan is the first to leave. His dad meets him in the lobby and whisks him out of the arena. Mike and I go back to the rink for a quick glimpse at the schedule for our next game. Brad and Tommy are already there.

"He's right but we couldn't move the lines faster," Brad replies on hearing what Ryan's dad thought. "We told everyone we won't shift when the puck's in our end. You even put it in writing."

I thought it was a relatively close game but now, I do recall some shifts where the puck spent a long time in our end. And there's no way I want to change lines then.

When we get home, I revisit the tournament Web site to double-check the rules and schedule. I confirm there's no possible way for us to miss the playoffs provided we win our next two games. Of the two possible times for the first playoff, neither would work with a meal. We'll have to make the semi-finals to do that. It reminds me when I first looked at the schedule, I hoped we'd finish in the top two and get the first round bye. That would've been ideal—a playoff win followed by a team lunch. It doesn't look too probable now.

Our game tomorrow is at St. Michael's Arena. My mother attended a fair number of games there. She grew up in Toronto and her all-girls school exchanged dances with the all-boys St. Mike's. She actually knew most of the players, at a time when St. Mike's was a major force in junior hockey.

I make sure we arrive an hour early since I want to look around the arena. Walking in, I notice the renovations completed since my mother's time—after all, it's still home to the Junior A St. Michael's Majors—but the historic wooden beams remain and, a few steps in, there's the St. Mike's Wall of Fame. The names and pictures of their most famous alumni hang here. It's a veritable who's who of Canadian hockey.

"Hey Mike, see this guy," I say, pointing to Dave Keon.

He reads the name. "Yeah," he replies in a surprised tone. "He's the guy I remind you of."

It's true. To me, Mike's fast and two-way, just like Keon.

"Whoa. Tim Horton played hockey?" he asks, his eyes widening as he sees the photo of the Leafs' famous number seven, before his doughnut days.

"Yeah. I told you that."

"No you didn't."

"Yes I did."

Normally, this would turn into one of those father-son yes I did/no you didn't conversations, but there's too many names and pictures for us to pore over. I'm stuck with the older photos, the faces of my youth—Mahovlich, Cheevers, Duff and Walton—while Mike looks at the more recent names like Lindros, Burke and Tocchet.

"See this guy?" I say, pointing to 'Red' Kelly. "Your grandmother actually went out with him." It's funny. The stories I'd largely ignored when my mother told them were now coming back fast and furious.

"Grandma went on a date with him?"

"Yup. He had red hair—that's why they called him 'Red.'"

"Did any one call you 'Red'?"

"Not really. Just a few old guys."

"Did grandma go out with anyone else?"

"I can't remember. She knew Mahovlich. I know she danced with Tim Horton. She says he was real quiet. Hardly spoke at all."

I could've spent the day there. I collected hockey cards and most of these pictures were in my collection. But as the younger boys arrive, I'm reminded there's a game to coach.

The hallways back to the dressing room are narrow and meander left, right, up and down. The kids love them. They're racing everywhere, taking great joy in the subterranean network.

The dressing room we're given is perfect—small, narrow with an empty spot on the wall where it looks like a wood stove sat fifty years ago. It's not hard to imagine the faces from the Wall of Fame, seated on either bench, facing each other, listening to the coach barking out his pre-game orders, as he walks up and down the room.

"The benches you're sitting on," I start, once everyone's dressed and ready to go, "are the exact same benches Dave Keon, Tim Horton and Eric Lindros sat on. All the best players in Canada have played in this arena. Bobby Orr, Wayne Gretzky. Their names aren't on that wall but they played here. It would be impossible to be a great Canadian hockey player and never play in St. Mike's. Only the best play in this arena. Now it's your turn."

The room is quiet. They're all looking directly at me. Mike's smiling, Turner's eyes are dancing; they can't wait. Ryan, Travis and Tommy look serious, focused—in their own way, just as ready.

"So I want you to think. I want you to pretend you're one of those players listening to his coach. What do you think the coach said? What do you think the player heard?" I pause briefly. The room is silent. "Think the coach told them to get the puck in front of the other team's net?"

Turner quickly nods.

"Think he told them to shoot the puck up the boards?"

Now Braeden's nodding.

"So what made them great? Why are they up on that Wall of Fame?"

"Because they did it," replies Mike, wryly.

"They tried their hardest," adds Travis.

"You got it. So boys, today it's your chance: your chance to play like Keon, Orr, Horton, Gretzky, Lindros and all those guys. On the very same ice they played on. So let's get out there and show them who the greatest kids in our town are. Alright?"

"Yeah," they shout in unison as they all jump up and head for the ice.

Brad's smiling as we follow them out. "I'm looking forward to this," he says.

The ice is perfect. It's so flat and clean you can almost see your reflection in it. We're missing Justin, but I've left the boys in their usual positions and will simply rotate Mike and Travis at centre. It means they'll have to take every second shift, but based on the energy they show in practice, I'm sure they can take it.

The puck drops and, like yesterday, the early signs are we can play with this team. But once again, after only three minutes, they've got the lead. This time however, we answer right back. Mike picks up the puck just outside our blue line and dekes around three of their players before wristing the puck, stick side, into the mesh. Finally, our boys have something to cheer about.

There aren't as many end-to-end plays as yesterday and no breakaways. It's a choppy game with possession changing constantly. Neither team is able to shake the other for long. But as the period winds down, we give the puck away in our zone and it costs us. One of their bigger forwards shoots high and hard over Tommy's glove to give them the lead again.

The team we're facing is an all-star team and reputedly better than the one we faced yesterday. Soon into the second period, it appears they're wearing us down. The puck spends more time in our zone and less in theirs. Halfway through, they cash in again.

"Come on guys," I say on the bench. "Don't give up. We can get back into this. Don't forget, this is the best rink in Canada, where all the best players have played. They wouldn't give up, would they?"

It's a risky thing to say but it pays immediate dividends. Mike takes the next faceoff and is all over them. Even when he loses the puck, he instantly goes back at them, anticipating their moves. He strips a defenceman of the puck and fires from the faceoff circle. The goalie catches a piece of it, but it slides toward the goal line. Kevin rushes the net and slams it in. We're back in the game.

The goal lifts our spirits but it's not long before the puck is once again trapped in our zone. Tommy's making saves but our clearing shots go straight to their defencemen who immediately fire them back toward our net. By the end of the period, entire shifts are being spent in our zone.

The third period starts. I've asked Travis to pay more attention to getting the puck out of our end, even to dump it out if he has to. His first clearing attempt is an icing so the faceoff comes right back. However, two minutes in, Mike's out and working his magic again. He steals the puck from their centre in the neutral zone and wheels back into their end. He dekes one defenceman and takes his shot from the hash marks. The goalie makes a pad save but the rebound comes straight to Will who flips it over him. We're tied. The all-stars' bench, adjacent to ours, suddenly has two very animated coaches shouting at their players.

Mike comes off and in mere seconds, the tide changes. They win the faceoff, take the puck straight into our zone and score.

"Don't worry guys, we can get it back." It's something you have to say as the coach, even when you don't believe it. This feels like one of those goals that finish a game.

A minute later, Travis takes a slashing penalty. Mike goes out to kill the penalty and continues his strong play. It occurs to me this might be the best I've ever seen him. He stays out for the entire penalty and if not for some bad luck, might've scored the equalizer. Travis returns rejuvenated after his penalty, and plays his best shift of the game. We get the only shot and keep the puck out of our end. We change lines at the faceoff and send Mike out again. The coach pulls his defence to the bench.

"You cover that number eight," he barks as he holds onto

their cages. "I don't care what he does, I don't care where he goes, stay with him. Okay? Both of you. You got that?"

Number eight is Mike. Hearing his strategy makes me angry. It's one of those things I would never do. I've thought about it before, but frankly, I'd rather lose than gang up on a kid with talent. It's pathetic to watch a grown man, with a team of his league's best players, instruct two players to forget their positions and shadow another kid. Even if the target weren't my son.

But soon after the puck drops, the two players follow their orders and skate close to Mike for the entire shift. Thankfully, there's no slashing of ankles or hands. Mike does get the puck a few times, but they close in on him fast. He passes off and his wingers get shots, but none hit the mark.

The all-stars add two more goals, and give Mike the MVP puck. With two losses in two games, we're officially out of the playoffs. On the way out, the Wall of Fame seems to have lost its lustre. Two other teams our age play after us. Watching only a bit of their game, I'm positive we'd beat either one.

I ask a tournament organizer for a program and he hands me his copy. Then he asks which team my son plays for.

"The Cougars. Actually, I'm the coach."

"You're kidding, the blue team? Wow. You nearly beat those guys. And they're good. We couldn't believe it. Way to go."

It's hard to muster a smile but I thank him. The drive home is quiet. I tell Mike how well he played but neither one of us talks much. For the first half of the journey I think about how I actually thought we had a chance of winning this tournament. Then it occurs to me someone in this van played his heart out today, and lost. After I labelled the game as something special.

"I'm really proud of you," I say, out of the blue. "If I had a team full of Mikes, we'd have killed them."

He laughs, but in a short, cut off way. "Thanks."

Life doesn't have Cinderella endings and unfortunately, trying your hardest doesn't always carry the day. It's a lesson everyone learns, but when it's your own kid, you wish he could learn it when he's older.

Our third game is against another group of all-stars who lost to the same teams we did. For the last twenty-four hours, the thought that's been running through my mind is we're too good to lose all three games. I've tried to think of what I could do to help our guys salvage a win. The only thing I've come up with is to anticipate the play as best as I can and make sure the kids are in position.

Once the puck drops, it's clear the two teams are evenly matched and neither one wants to go home winless. Turner's skating hard and is as tenacious as ever. His hard work gets us the first goal but they tie it shortly after. Travis, too, is playing well and converts a nice feed from Joel, three minutes later. As if on cue, our opponents tie it again three minutes after that. Midway through the second I feel my voice getting hoarse. I'm shouting more than I have in any game all season, trying to read the play and warn the kids. We fall behind on a goalmouth scramble but with twenty-five seconds left in the second period, Turner strips the puck off one of their players and finds the mesh again. One period to go, winner take all.

The kids on both teams sense this is the game they can win. Desperation sets in. With each passing minute, the play and tension elevates. I can feel my heart pounding as if it's at least two inches outside my chest. Just when it looks like no one will break through, Mike intercepts a pass in the neutral zone. He tips it past their last defence and races in all alone. From the bench I can see the mesh on the left side. Mike sees it too and picks the corner beautifully. We're up by one with four minutes to go.

I feel that will do it, but once the puck drops it quickly appears otherwise. The all-star team races into our zone, desperate for a goal. Joel, Justin, Braeden, Simon and Luke decide to make a stand. Cougars bravely dive in front of shots, lunge after players from behind and try to clear the puck any time they get near it. But the all-stars' defence are playing well and blocking our shots at the blue line. The puck doesn't leave our zone during the final two minutes but, miraculously, we hold them off. When the buzzer sounds, kids and coaches scream in celebration. It was a war, but we won it.

"Let's hear those cheers," I yell as we enter the dressing room, my voice cracking. "Hip, hip . . ."

"Hooray!"

"Come on guys, you won, let's hear it. Hip, hip . . ."

"Hooray!"

"Ah, you can do better than that. You just beat an all-star team! Hip, hip . . ."

"HOORAY!!!"

The loudest hooray of the season matches the smiles everywhere. And this time, parents and kids alike hang around well after the game has ended, recounting great plays by their kids, by other kids. We're not in the playoffs but we're a good team after all. At least to this biased group.

Two days later, the final results for the tournament are posted on the association's Web site. The two teams that beat us trounced every other team they played and met in the finals. We did better than anyone in terms of scoring. The second best against the powerhouses was the team we played third. So that was it—judging by goals scored, the four best teams in the tournament were all in our division. Lucky us. My e-mail to the team informs them of this truthful rationalization. I picked a tournament I thought we'd be competitive in. On the basis of play, we were, but based on the score, we weren't. I wanted to bring the team closer together as a group, but given the game times and results, it didn't happen. We didn't even have time for a team meal.

Strangely, I don't feel all that bad. It would've been nice to win but it wasn't as if we folded our tents. We're a good team. I know it. My gut tells me we'll be fine. Good things will come for this team. I'm sure of it.

THE GRETZKY

Early in January I received an e-mail from the organizer of the Walter Gretzky Tournament in Brantford. He was short a team and wondered if we were interested. Our opponents would all be house league but we'd have to play in the Novice division with teams a year older. I hadn't planned on another tournament but when he offered to discount the fee, I jumped at it.

"On some teams, every kid will be nine years old," I explained to the parents, "On others, it'll be half and half. Some will be just like us—all eight-year-olds. But it's strictly house league. There's no all-stars in this one."

The tournament doesn't start for another week and in the meantime, we have the Hawks to contend with. We're in first place with six games to go. As Brad says: "It's time we thought about getting the boys some hardware."

There are three trophies up for grabs—one each to the first place team, the playoff champion and the playoff runner-up. The first place trophy is the nicest and reads *League Champions* at the bottom. We'll have to win most and possibly all six of our remaining games to clinch that trophy.

The Hawks boast two of the top ten scorers, as well as several other players I know are good. Even though we won our first game against them, they outskated us. We're better now, but factor in the Christmas season when kids social and sleeping patterns go haywire, and it has the feel of a game we could easily lose.

Our dressing room beforehand is quiet. Everyone's ready early, sitting on the benches, waiting patiently. I fill out the game sheet and take it to the Hawks' room.

"Kill the Cougars. Kill the Cougars," screams the coach's son, standing on one of the benches. His teammates shout and pump their fists in the air. It becomes a warlike chant, with every kid in the room joining in. As I hand over the game sheet, the coach smiles. I wish him luck and leave quickly.

"Hey guys," I announce back in our room. "I got to tell you. The Hawks are ready and they want to win. We better play our hardest." I add the usual strategy review, highlighting the lessons we learned in the tournament—primarily, the importance of working as a team in our own end. I try to instigate some rah-rah cheering of my own, but we file out of the room as staid and sober as ever. We're going to get killed, I think to myself.

The next thirty-two minutes add a valuable lesson to my education in how to coach a kids' hockey team. It was embarrassing: five-nothing after the first, eight-nothing after the second. That's when I went to our new convenor, Dennis, and asked what I should do.

He had no idea. "This should be a lot closer," he said.

It wasn't. The timekeeper was so busy writing down goals and assists he missed one. We absolutely destroyed them. All lines scored at least two goals and Mike had a field day, getting nine points, one shy of Darryl Sittler's NHL record. For the third period, we made a rule that all players on the ice had to touch the puck before anyone could shoot. We scored six more. The final was fourteen-two. The Hawks played their game in the dressing room; we played ours on the ice.

It's never a great feeling to coach a one-sided game, but if it had to occur, this was good timing. Any confidence the boys lost playing in Toronto had no doubt returned. "How many points did you get?" was a common question heard between players after the game. Ryan summed it up best when, grinning ear to ear, he replied: "I can't remember."

Combining the Gretzky tournament with our regular season game means we'll play four games over the weekend, possibly more if we make the playoffs. It allows me to deal with a situation that has cropped up in goal.

Andrew is a nice kid who was far and away the most talkative player on the bench when the season started. Trouble was, he would talk about anything except hockey, and always when the play was on. At first, I dutifully listened, but the stories got longer. I started trying to watch the play while I listened to Andrew, but I think he got the sense I wasn't completely immersed in what his teacher said, or what happened to a friend he had last year. When he asked if brownies were my favourite dessert too, and got nary a response, our conversations ended. He switched to teammates and I haven't heard much from him since—at least during the game.

After the game, he asks the same question and smiles no matter what my response: "Will I be goalie next week?"

Andrew's father represents the company that sponsored our team. When he delivered the cheque to the league office, he asked if Andrew could play net. They said okay but failed to label him as a goalie. He landed on our team as a skater. Tommy was already our full-time goalie.

Fortunately, both sets of parents were cooperative. We struck a deal whereby we'd give Tommy two games in net, then Andrew one. In December, we gave Tommy a string of games to prepare him for the Toronto tournament. It's now Andrew's turn but Tommy is on a roll. He's improving with every game, is a bona fide star of the team and doesn't want to come out.

The upcoming four games will provide a solution: they'll each play two. Tommy will play tournament games Friday morning and Saturday afternoon; Andrew will play the Friday afternoon game and our league match Saturday morning. It's against the team currently in last place, so it should be a game he can handle.

Travis' parents are both busy Friday so he will ride with us. The drive is mostly four-lane highway with few sights on the way.

"Hey, that's the church my parents got married in," says Travis, as we drive through Hamilton, passing by the Cathedral of Christ the King, high on the Mountain.

"It's nice," replies Mike. The two get along fine the whole way, and fortunately, the weather is perfect. We arrive more than an hour early.

Signs erase any doubt about Brantford's most famous son. We exit at the Wayne Gretzky Parkway and make our way to the tournament's main venue: the Wayne Gretzky Sports Complex. We collect the form for the kids to sign, the game sheet and a summary of the rules for the tournament. I'm told both of today's games are against Brantford Novice teams, which means half the boys are a year older. During the pre-game I remind our guys it doesn't matter who we're playing, the strategy is the same. Get the puck in front of the other team's net, and keep it away from your own.

Watching the warm-up, I'm relieved to see no really big boys on the other team. As play starts, it quickly becomes clear size won't be a factor. We score on our first, third, fifth, sixth and seventh shifts, and with no goals against. Early in the second period, I move our best forwards back to defence and our defencemen up to forward. The boys love it. We rotate centres every shift. But still, we continue scoring. In fact, it's almost worse. Kids who normally don't score, sense a real opportunity for goals and play harder. At game's end the scoresheet reads twelve-nothing. The dressing room is boisterous.

There's three and a half hours between games so we all head to a nearby roadhouse. We seat the kids at one table, with the adults next door. The boys are fairly civilized for the first half hour but predictably, once they finish eating, restlessness sets in. A few head toward the front of the restaurant to check out a TV; three more head for the washroom. I rise to follow them but am distracted by three boys using their spoons to catapult the left-over food from the table. Fortunately, there's a small play area at the back of the restaurant. We corral the kids there while the adults finish eating.

Joel lets it slip his birthday's coming up so a dad jokingly asks our waitress if they have anything special for the birthday boy. A few minutes later, a parade of waiters and waitresses appear. It's a great diversion. The woman in the lead carries a small cake but right behind her, another holds a furry hat with gigantic moose antlers sticking out its sides. No one can keep a straight face when the hat is placed on Joel's head—at least five sizes too big. First it falls to his left, then to his right. Once balanced, he tries valiantly to keep his head perfectly still while the staff and kids sing away. A camera flashes, capturing an ear-to-ear grin under a moose head.

"Hey, it's the coach's birthday too," jokes Justin's dad.

"Sorry sir," replies the waitress, "but there's a limit of one cake per party."

The afternoon game is only marginally more competitive. Our opponents get three shots this time, one more than this morning's. Andrew doesn't seem nervous but two of the shots get by him. Still, we send eleven into the other net, making the day's aggregate twenty-three to two.

As I walk back to the dressing room, I'm concerned the blowouts will impact our league game. The boys talk with their friends at school and know we're playing the last place team.

"Guys," I announce in the dressing room, "don't forget we play at eight tomorrow morning, and that's the game we need to win. The Sharks have been playing well lately. We'd better be ready."

"You always say the other team's playing well," replies Braeden, grinning.

"Because it's true," echoes Brad. "We're getting close. You don't want to miss out on first place because of one lousy game. Especially against a team we should beat."

It's tough to tell if the message gets through, but a few of them nod. We pack up quickly and get in the van for the ride home.

"There's the church your parents got married in," says Mike, as we approach the cathedral from the Brantford side.

"Hey, yeah," says Travis. They talk about school, with not so much a mention of anything related to hockey. It seems mildly odd since many parents consider them the two best players in the league.

A little over twelve hours later, we're back in an arena, but this one's in our hometown.

"It's great we won yesterday," I announce in my pre-game talk, "but this is our league game, the one that really matters."

The game is almost as one-sided as in the tournament, except for one significant factor. Their goalie is the best in the league; Andrew's struggling. Shots at the end of the first period are fifteen-one for us, but the score is tied. By the end of the second, we're up three-one and Andrew's made his first save. But with five minutes left in the game, we're even at four-four. We've taken at least forty shots. Then one of their players makes an innocent looking clearing shot out of his zone on a line change. The puck heads for our goal. Andrew's standing in the middle of the net, watching. He doesn't so much as move. The puck slides ever closer with no sign Andrew's going to stop it.

"Andrew, the puck!" I yell. He remains motionless.

The puck slides through the crease and grazes the outside of the post with Andrew still entranced. Braeden arrives to shoot it up the boards, out of harm's way.

"Can you believe that?" I ask Brad, standing at the end of the bench.

"Pretty scary," he replies.

Two minutes later, Travis swerves in from the blue line and lets one of his patented wrist shots go to clinch the victory, five-four. It was a game we dominated. Over thirty-two minutes, they had a grand total of seven shots. None were dangerous. In practice this week, Andrew pulled himself out of goal three times, claiming he needed a break from all the shots. It's pretty clear who our goalie has to be from here on.

As I drive to Brantford, I can't get the shot out of my head. It's not exasperation with Andrew. It's the conversation coming up with his dad that's bugging me. All season long, his father's portrayed Andrew as a boy who lives to play goal. He idolizes Curtis Joseph. When Andrew is in net, parents and son thank me for giving him the opportunity. When Andrew plays any other position, their comments are little more than "he's much better in goal." And now, I have no choice. There's no way I can let Andrew play any more games in net. It wouldn't be fair to the team, or to Tommy, who works much harder and is much better.

"Hey, there's the church Travis' parents got married in," says Mike, as we drive by what is becoming a personal Hamilton landmark.

"How'd you know that?" asks my wife.

We all share a laugh on the things kids remember.

Arriving at the Brantford arena, I learn we've already made the playoffs and therefore are guaranteed two more games on Sunday, as well as some sort of trophy or plaque.

"Did you get a look at the trophies?" asks George, hearing the news.

"Yeah, they're this big," I answer, holding my arms three feet apart, before dropping one to show the fingers on my other, two inches high. He laughs.

"Which is it?" asks Travis.

"I didn't see them," I answer, with a wink. "I'm sure they're fine."

Our third game is peculiar. Although not because our opponents are a year older and, in truth, a Select team. Rather, there's a spot in the ice about two feet by three feet that doesn't fully freeze after the flood. In the first period, it's located just outside our blue line, a spot we go through time and time again. More accurately, it's a spot we try to go through. When a frozen puck hits water, it stops. The puck carrier doesn't. And for whatever reason, we're drawn to this spot like a ship to the Bermuda triangle. Our scoring chances suffer the same fate many Atlantic schooners did. By the time the boys and I have figured out the problem, we're down two-nothing. From that point on, the game is a goalless draw so we finish second in our group. That means we'll play the first place team from the other division tomorrow morning.

Andrew's family is taking him skiing for the day so Tommy will get both playoff games in goal without me having to say anything.

Sunday starts clear and sunny. The drive to Brantford is easy. "Hey, there's the church . . ."

"We know Mike. Everyone knows. Travis' parents were married there."

"It is a nice church."

When we walk into the Wayne Gretzky complex, Ryan's dad is waiting. "Have you heard about this team we're playing?" he asks. "They've been killing everyone."

It doesn't bother me. After all, two of our games were blowouts. At the tournament office I meet the other coach. After comparing notes it sounds like the only issue will be age. Their kids were born in 1992, a year earlier than our 1993's.

Arriving back in our dressing room, I'm quickly reminded of the new dimension that's been added to our team. Patrick's been relatively well behaved since the early season. There's been the odd joke or prank but he's nowhere near as disruptive as he started out. However, a few weeks ago, his family rented the movie *Remember the Titans*. Patrick loved the team song. In fact, he felt it was good enough to be our team song. He's been singing it unabashedly, loud and clear, ever since. It's a catchy tune and though no one's joined in, I've overheard a few players humming or singing it to themselves on their way out of the dressing room. Today, at our first playoff game, Patrick decides to take it public. As we skate our warm-up, he's in full voice. Kevin joins in. The two make every effort to be heard, and they succeed. Their eight-year-old voices reverberate throughout the entire arena. Smiles instantly form on the faces of parents gathering near the glass.

"We may not be great hockey players," I say to the opposition coaches as we walk to the bench, "but we can sing."

We should've stayed with the singing, particularly Patrick. Although the score is only two-nothing at the end of the first period, this is a good team of nine-year-olds we're playing. The extra inches make their strides that much longer and their skating that much quicker. The few extra pounds make their shots that much harder. We're okay in scrums when the play is close, but in the open ice we can't catch them when they have the puck, and can't shake them when we do. One of their players wheels by Patrick midway through the period. All Patrick can do is wave at him. But he waves with both hands on his stick and hits the boy in the back. As luck would have it, Will crosses the player's path at exactly the same time. The boy veers, falls and slides into the boards. It happens so quickly it looks like Patrick cross-checked the boy into the boards. The ref instantly raises his hand and gives Patrick the mandatory suspension. He escorts him to the door on the other side of the rink while everyone on the bench watches. Patrick stands by the door for a couple of minutes until his dad arrives to take him to the dressing room. It's the first penalty he's ever received.

After a brief conference with the linesman, the ref arrives at our bench. He says one of the players on the ice will have to serve Patrick's penalty. Will is closest so I ask if he'd mind. He starts crying.

"It's okay, you don't have to," I quickly tell him. I've never seen Will do anything but smile. In fact he smiles so much, you find yourself smiling every time you see him. This isn't like him at all.

"Hey Turner, can you go?" asks Brad.

Turner heads for the penalty box. Will keeps crying.

"Maybe he thinks he got a penalty."

"You didn't do anything wrong," I assure him. "Patrick got kicked out of the game and we need someone to sit in the penalty box for a couple of minutes. It has nothing to do with you."

Will won't stop crying. I try to get him to drink some water but he doesn't want any. Play resumes, and slowly Will gathers his composure, but he still won't talk.

We're getting shots, but mostly long range, fired in desperation, when the shooter is about to lose the puck. Unfortunately, in the second period, the bottom falls out. They put seven more past Tommy to make it nine-nothing heading into the third.

"I want you to know, we're not trying to run up the score," says the opposition coach, leaning over the glass between the benches.

"I wish we could give you more of a match," I tell him.

He shrugs. "You're doing better than anyone else. Your guys are just smaller."

It's not much comfort. I tell the boys to forget about winning, but instead, to concentrate on each shift, and see if we can break the shutout. "No one's scored on these guys," I say. "Let's see if we can."

Whether it's the pep talk, or the other team backing off, we do get more chances, but none go past their goalie. In the end, we suffer the same fate everyone else has.

After the game, the boys are upset. The parents rationalize, speaking of age differences and number of practices. But to players and coaches, a loss is a loss is a loss. It never feels good. Will finally manages to tell me what was bugging him. He felt he caused the whole problem with Patrick, and was the reason Patrick got kicked out. I assure him that wasn't the case. He smiles and says he knows that now.

We've qualified for the Consolation Final, to be played in a couple of hours—too tight to organize a team lunch. Some stay at the arena, grab a sandwich at the cafeteria and watch the hockey, while others, including us, head for the fast food strip. On our return, a kid flies by saying Walter Gretzky is signing autographs in the observation area upstairs. It's quickly the talk of the team. The boys drop their equipment bags and run up the nearest staircase.

The Great One's dad is seated at a small table in the corner of a large room. He's affably signing posters, sweaters, notebooks—whatever he's asked—as a huge mob of kids and parents surround him. He does it well, not in the least intimidated by the numbers. He chats with each and every autograph seeker, asking them about school, hockey, whatever. He smiles, laughs, teases. The kids walk away beaming. An hour later, our boys are showing off their signatures as they get ready for the game.

It turns out the team we're playing in the final might be our most evenly matched. They're a Select team from a smaller centre, the same age as us. Their record in the tournament is identical.

The boys are calm before the game but parents are excited. Many give their son an extra pep talk. Andrew's family has hurried back from skiing to make the final, but without his goalie equipment so he'll play defence. I wasn't nervous before, but seeing the adults behave this way puts me a little on edge. I suppose it still is a championship, albeit a consolation one.

The game starts fast and stays that way. Being Select, their fifteen players are more or less equal in talent. We have both the best and worst players on the ice. It's an even game but we score the first, second and third goals of the game. With four minutes left, we look to have the game sewn up. Then their best line puts together a nice three-way passing play that clicks to make it three-one. On the ensuing faceoff, they dump it into our end, on Andrew's side. Whether it's nerves or the skiing, he's played indifferently all game. He skates toward the puck at half speed and is easily beaten by their winger, who takes it straight to our goal. It's three-two with three minutes left.

"Why doesn't Andrew try?" asks a boy on the bench. He's the third boy to ask the same question.

The two goals in thirty seconds have given their team a new dose of energy. They storm our end but the Cougars have gathered resolve of their own. No shots make it to Tommy over the next minute. Then, we reverse the pressure, forcing the play, winning two more faceoffs back in their end. The buzzer sounds before they have a chance to pull their goalie. The boys pile on top of each other, outside our goal. We've won.

Surprisingly, the refs escort us off the ice without any kind of trophy presentation. I know we're supposed to receive them, so while the team heads to the dressing room I go to the tournament office to ask.

"Your game is over?" asks the surprised tournament organizer. "Sorry, I guess we missed you. I'll find Walter and meet you in the dressing room."

He scurries out of the office. Walter *Gretzky*, I wonder. Coming to our dressing room? Surely there couldn't be another Walter.

Five minutes later, a diminutive man with a lot of energy bounces into the crowd of kids and parents in our dressing room. Walter Gretzky—in the flesh.

"Hello everyone. Sorry we're late," he says. "You guys are too fast for us."

The President of Brantford Minor Hockey follows him in, carrying a large cardboard box. One by one, Walter Gretzky shakes the hand of each player and hands him a plaque reading *Novice Consolation Champs*. He pauses for a picture with each boy. He even allows multiple photos for those who want them. Finally, we all get together and pose for the group shot. Flashes go off like fireworks as each family gets a copy.

The gang breaks up but the main attraction is still chatting, with me and with the kids. He asks about our league, our town. He appears to be in no hurry and, naturally, neither are we.

"We even have a team song," blurts out Patrick.

"You what?"

No more encouragement is needed. Patrick starts it off but the fifteen others immediately prove they know the words too.

> Everywhere we go (everywhere we go)
> People want to know (people want to know)
> Who we are (who we are)
> So we tell them (so we tell them)
> We are the Cougars (we are the Cougars)
> The mighty, mighty Cougars (the mighty, mighty Cougars)

Walter Gretzky doesn't move. He listens to every word, every note. It occurs to me other playoff games are going on and they could be waiting for him. But he allows the kids to finish, waiting patiently to a song that suddenly strikes me as a little lengthy.

"What great singers you are," he says when the chorus finally ends.

"We have to go now guys," interjects the President, "the other team is waiting."

The two leave to a chorus of byes and thank yous. I follow them out.

"Thanks an awful lot," I say, catching up to Walter Gretzky in the hallway and extending my hand. "You really made those kids happy. That was nice of you."

"No problem." he replies. "Good luck with your season."

I thank him once more as he's ushered to the next dressing room and another group of kids and parents. It's a great end to a great tournament. There's no doubt this one has brought our team much closer.

"Hey! There's the church Travis' parents were married in," I say as we pass the cathedral, lit up in the night sky.

"Dad. Give it a rest."

The next day I drop off a copy of the Walter Gretzky team photo at the town press. They publish it a week later, complete with players' and coaches' names. I get congratulated every time I'm in an arena for almost the next month. It's hard not to feel proud.

FIRST PLACE SHOWDOWN

The Monday following our tournament success, I send an e-mail to the team explaining exactly what we have to do to clinch first place. Dennis, who took over as convenor when Rose became too busy, has told us our lead is now three points. I thought the standings were much tighter but Dennis insists they're correct as posted. Regardless, we're in the driver's seat.

"Just so you know," starts Brad as he and I head out onto the practice ice, "the league has a rule that requires any suspension received in a tournament to be served in league play."

I look it up and sure enough, Patrick will have to miss a league match, in addition to the tournament game he's already missed. On hearing the news, his dad's upset—he feels Patrick didn't mean to do it, barely touched the other player and sitting out the tournament championship is punishment enough. To make matters worse, this week's game is Photo Day. Patrick will have to get all his equipment on for the team picture, then take it off, alone, in the dressing room. I check with Dennis. He confirms the rule, but understands the dilemma and says he'll take it up with the VP House League.

In the meantime, Patrick's dad talks to the league office. Someone there tells him if the coach hadn't opened his big mouth, no one would've known.

"That person should be fired," says Brad, on hearing the latest tidbit, "What an unbelievable thing to say. Are there any other rules we can ignore? You can bet your bottom dollar, if we win the league and someone finds out we had an ineligible player, that person would be the first to take it away from us."

I'd figured that out on my own. The other rule I came across was any coach who knowingly uses an ineligible player, gets an automatic three-game suspension and must attend a discipline hearing. Wouldn't that look good on my resume?

A few days later, the VP House League calls me. He congratulates us on our performance in the Gretzky, then tells me Patrick can play on Photo Day, provided he serves his suspension during the following week. Patrick's dad is gratified. He'll use the Saturday off to take Patrick to his grandmother's.

We're practicing twice a week now—our regular half-ice plus a full sheet we buy on our own. The latter is a huge hit with kids and parents alike, despite its early start—quarter to seven every Wednesday morning. There's no one on the ice before or after so the arena crew lets us start and finish when we want. I let the boys goof around before and scrimmage after. Most days we have Cougars on the ice for a full ninety minutes.

With the extra space, we've let a few more dads join in. It allows us to do more with the kids. I've made it clear I don't want any adult coming out just to prove they're the best eight-year-old and so far, it's worked. The dads provide enough pressure to challenge the kids, while at the same time, back off sufficiently to allow the boys to succeed.

Braeden's granddad has also joined in, giving me hope I won't have to cease all movement when my kids grow up. He's one of the early birds, using the time before practice to give Braeden some pointers on shooting or stickhandling. It's great to see. Once the practice starts, he helps out as much as anyone, playing forward in some drills, defence in others.

The coaching clinic I attended in December has provided some good ideas for practice, primarily from a Hockey Canada book they handed out titled *Fun and Games*. It's a manual of seventy-three different games that can be used to teach particular skills. Each week we try something new but there's one we're playing every week: Raptors. The kids love it. Every skater except one—the raptor—starts out with a puck. Once the whistle blows, the raptor must take a puck off a skater and fire it into the open net. The skater who lost his puck now becomes a raptor too. The game continues until all the pucks are in the net. Few of the kids even realize how many skills the game is teaching them. Before we start, we review different ways to stick check. Then we talk about how to protect your puck from someone trying to take it away. As far as the kids know, all of this is for the sole purpose of getting better at Raptors. We often play for ten or fifteen minutes, which is a testament to the kids' fitness. With all the stops, starts and turns, it takes a lot of energy. But the big payoff has been in our games.

"Play like a raptor," I'll say on the bench. We do. In addition to becoming fast, we have also become a very aggressive forechecking team. I doubt any of our boys would know a forecheck from a blank cheque, but they know how to play like a raptor. And it means our opponents spend more time in their end than they'd like.

Another wrinkle we've added to make practices more interesting is something we call the "sneak play." Hockey aficionados would know it simply as a trailer play, but I figured a kid would rather be a sneak than a trailer. The forwards use the play when they enter the other team's zone. Instead of coming in three-across, one forward curls in behind the other two. He's almost always wide open. Will, possibly the most innocent looking boy on the team, really likes the sneak play. Although he hasn't used it in a game yet, we're hoping our opponents will soon get a lesson they can apply to life outside hockey: beware the innocent looking ones.

On Photo Day we play the Wildcats, a team we have to play well against to win. Fortunately, we don't miss a beat, continuing the form that won us our Gretzky plaque, and emerge with a four-two victory. The teams behind us win too, so our three-point cushion stays the same.

Early in the week, I receive an e-mail from Dennis. Sure enough, some of the games were entered incorrectly and he's had to redo the standings. We are in first place, but only by two points. And the team chasing us isn't the one he thought it was. It's the team we're playing this week, our old friends, the Giants.

Given how well we're playing, and the fact we beat them four-one in December, I'm not terribly worried. However, at our mid-week practice, only eight boys show up. I was expecting fourteen. It doesn't make sense. I know the kids prefer these practices to any other. Kevin's mom told me he actually wakes them up on Wednesday mornings. Today, Kevin is among the missing.

"What gives?" I ask Brad at centre ice. "Saturday's the big game. Why isn't anyone here?"

He shrugs. There aren't even enough players for a decent game of Raptors. Instead we play dads versus kids in a scrimmage. It's fun but we could've used a real practice.

When I get home, the explanations pour in. Ryan, Kevin, Luke, Joel, Justin, Robert and Connor are all down with the flu. Reading the details, it sounds grim—fevers, sore throats, nausea. Our game is at 7 A.M. in three days. I can't see everyone recovering. The question is: how many will play and what lineup should I use.

I double-check the standings. If we lose, we'll be tied with the Giants. The league has rules to decide which team finishes first.

The first tiebreaker is based on wins, but assuming we both win our final game, we'll each have eleven wins, five losses and three ties. The second tiebreaker is who won the most games between the two teams. That would be the Giants. So if we lose this game, we lose first place.

The league also has rules when you're missing players. I can't just pick which positions get more shifts. If we're missing one or two players, I have to give the extra ice time to my defence. But if I'm missing three—a distinct possibility—I can go with two centres, four defence and six wingers. That means I could rotate Mike and Travis at centre for the entire game. They're currently the league's number one and number three scorers. I can live with that.

I ask the parents of the "sicklies" to give me a heads-up on Friday as to whether their son will make it to the game or not. Emphasizing it's purely a lineup issue, I tell them not to pressure their child to come if he's ill. We're also playing an exhibition game that night. It's ironic. We were offered the game a couple of weeks ago. I didn't want to do it, but asked the parents as an afterthought. Virtually every parent was in favour of playing. With half the team questionable for our league game, I can't see us getting many for an exhibition.

Our league practice falls on Friday night and hardly anyone shows. Still, no one's told me they're going to miss tomorrow's game. I send around another e-mail when I get home asking for updates. No one replies.

Next morning, Mike and I arrive at the arena by six thirty. Ryan's already there, fully dressed and waiting patiently.

"How's he feeling?" I ask his dad.

"He should be okay," he replies, emphasizing the word *should*. "He has a bit of a cough."

Ryan looks sullen. He sits completely still, looking straight ahead. In walk Luke, Joel and Connor. Their parents too claim the boys are ready to play.

Justin arrives in good spirits. "You may want to keep an eye on him," says his dad. "He seems okay but he hasn't been to school all week."

Ten minutes before game time, Kevin traipses in, his boots drag-stepping across the floor. He's fully dressed but his eyes are glassy. "He says he wants to play," claims his mom.

So much for planning to rotate Mike and Travis. Save for one—Robert, who's been our best defenceman of late—the entire team's here.

"Alright guys, this is it," I say in the pre-game speech. "Win this game, we get a trophy."

There's nothing unusual about the warm-up or the early shifts. But midway through the first, the coughing starts. First it's Ryan. Soon Justin joins in. Then Joel. George asks if he needs his puffer. Joel nods. As the second period starts, so does Luke's cough. Almost everyone sits down between shifts—something they've never done before. Kevin is the last to join the cough chorus, but makes up for his lateness by having the scratchiest and loudest of the bunch. As the second period ends, all you can hear on our bench is one cough after another. It's non-stop and it's ridiculous. Brad and I exchange glances. He's as appalled as I am.

We have six water bottles. I encourage the boys to drink after every shift and try to keep the ones used by the healthy kids separate from the sicklies'. Still, between watching the play, giving the boys pointers, and trying to remember which bottle I left where, there's no doubt a few more will join the infirmary in a day or two. As far as the game goes, the sicklies are next to useless. Their lungs simply won't allow them to skate hard. Few are able to last much beyond twenty seconds. Some just loaf around the ice watching the play, while others come off voluntarily, something else they've never done before.

The Giants carry the play and we're lucky to be down by one after the first. The puck spends most of the period in our zone.

Tommy, Travis, Braeden and Mike are all having good games. Unfortunately, they're on their own. With a minute left in the second, Braeden fires the puck out of our end off the boards. The carom carries perfectly to Travis and he's off. No one comes close to catching him and he fires that tough wrist shot of his, high glove side, into the mesh. We're still tied when the buzzer sounds to end the second. Whoever wins the third, gets the trophy.

"If you're not feeling well, stay off," I tell the sicklies. None do. Each assures me they're okay, then goes out and proves otherwise. The healthys are doing everything they can to get the advantage, but the Giants are playing well. We simply have too many players who can't keep up. Then, on a play reminiscent of his first goal, Travis picks up the puck outside our blue line, skating low and fast, swerving around the Giants' defence. They force him outside. He shoots. The puck stays low, something Mike's told me works better on the goalies in this league. It sure does this time. With a little over eight minutes to go, we've got the lead.

The goal lifts our team. Even the sicklies sense first place is in our grasp. They dig deeper for energy. Surprisingly, they find it. The play evens out. It's hard for either team to carry the puck much beyond the neutral zone. Once again however, the puck emerges from a scrum to find its way onto the stick of a speedy player. Unfortunately, the player is wearing black, and heads into our zone. His wrist shot is high and it's the Giants' turn to cheer. Five minutes left. It's two-two. Winner takes all.

Mike's out next and calmly skates to centre. Once the puck drops, he's anything but calm. Single-handedly he carries the puck into the Giants' zone, deking around their defence. He fires. The save is made. Another faceoff in their zone, a scrum and Mike emerges with it to shoot once again. Another save. The Giants try to clear, Mike cuts it off. He shoots again. It's off the post. Once again he cuts off the Giants' attempt to clear and fires from the outside hash marks. This time the Giants' goalie holds on to the puck for another faceoff. It's one of Mike's best shifts this season but we have to take him off. The game's still tied.

Travis takes to the ice. There's only a minute left but with both goals today, he's on his game. Unfortunately, there's no more magic. He rushes but the puck slides off his stick. The speediest of the Giants picks it up near his blue line, flies past our wingers and dekes our defence. He pulls the puck to his forehand and fires. Tommy makes the save but can't control the rebound. The Giants buzz the net with Tommy on his knees. I glance at the clock—fifteen seconds.

"Clear it. Fast," I shout. My heart is pounding. Cougars dive in desperation. The puck trickles to one of their players who shows he's smart under pressure. Rather than shoot, he passes across the crease to the Giants' top gun, number four. Tommy slides but he's too low. The Giant leans hard on his stick and fires. From the bench, my view is perfect. It's labelled—top corner, right side. Tommy appears to raise his mask ever so slightly toward the puck. It's enough. The puck nicks the top of his helmet then grazes the crossbar. It lands in open ice, out of anyone's reach. The buzzer sounds. Tie game.

"Did you mean to do that?" I ask in the dressing room after.

"Uh-huh," replies Tommy, matter-of-factly. "I saw it."

If he did, I don't know how. Regardless, everyone, including the sicklies, is smiling. They all want to know if a tie clinched it for us. It did, if the standings are right. Unfortunately, with all the mix-ups and week-to-week changes, I don't want to say anything till after our next game. By then I can check and double-check the results.

Our exhibition game that evening is a non-event except for the fact all the sicklies show up. They're just as inept as this morning, but no one wants to miss a hockey game. Between shifts, Kevin lies flat on the bench, eyes facing the ceiling. He asks George to take his gloves off. "T.J., feel his hands. He's burning up."

I ask Kevin if he's well enough to play. He sadly shakes his head so I motion to his parents in the stands. His father arrives a few minutes later. I explain the situation and leave Kevin with him.

"T.J.," the dad calls to me, after a brief talk with his son. "Kevin says he's fine. He can play." Kevin makes his way back onto the bench.

"You sure? He has a fever."

"He'll be fine," reiterates the dad. "You know kids and their hockey."

The father returns to the stands. I ask Kevin again if he's well enough to play. This time he nods, but his eyes are glassy. His expression is hardly enthusiastic. "Okay. But let's keep your shifts short, alright? I mean really short. And you come off if you're feeling sick, you hear me?" He manages a smile and nods.

Once again, I've split the water bottles into healthy and not. The kids are actually asking for "some of the healthy" when they come off. The coughing is just as pronounced as this morning, and the only players who can mount any kind of challenge are Tommy, Braeden, Travis and Mike. Unfortunately, we're playing a Select team with five solid players on the ice at all times. Most of the night is spent in our zone. We lose four-nothing but it would've been much worse had it not been for Tommy playing one of his best games. Even the opposition coach is impressed and tells him so in our dressing room after.

Monday morning arrives and Mike wakes up with a cough. I check his throat—it's scarlet. He's too sick for school. *New team rule,* I type in the subject line of an e-mail message. *If you're sick, stay home. Rgds, T.J.*

HOME ICE ADVANTAGE AND THE TRUTH ABOUT REFEREES

From the start of the season, we've known there would be no games played on the second weekend in February, due to an ice scheduling conflict. I've always felt the timing was lousy since it takes the kids off the ice, right before the playoffs. In December, I came across a Select tournament that very same weekend. It was less than an hour away and we'd get to play teams our own age. It seemed like a perfect fit so I signed us up. In late January, I received the information package. It asked me to submit a list of five names for a skills competition, as well as two names for an all-star game.

"An all-star game," exclaimed Mike, his eyes lighting up. "Will I get to play?"

It did sound like fun. Each player wears a special all-star jersey with his choice of number. For fifty dollars, he gets his name on the back and can keep it.

"I nominate Joel," replied George to an e-mail I sent requesting opinions from the other coaches, "he'll love the sweater."

I could see this was going to be a problem. What kid wouldn't want to play in an all-star game and get a personalized all-star jersey? Even if we tried to keep it secret, everyone will hear about it at the tournament. Mike is miles ahead in the scoring race so I can't see anyone disputing that pick. Joel is one of our top players but only seventh in team scoring. On the other hand, George bought the team practice jerseys, helps out on the ice and on the bench. What's the harm in letting Joel go as a thank you to George?

Dave didn't respond to my e-mail and later admits to "ducking it." Still, I wonder how he'd feel about Travis being passed over. Dave helps out at practice too.

Fortunately, when it comes to all-star games, there is a precedent. *In the spirit of the NHL,* I write in an e-mail to the team, *we'll hold a vote to determine which two Cougars go to the all-star game. Every player gets a first, second and third choice. No votes for yourself. The top two vote getters will go to the game.*

Two weeks later, I close off the voting. Mike wins handily. Travis is runner-up and Ryan, Joel and Turner form a virtual tie for third. So Mike and Travis will be our all-stars. Ryan, Joel, Turner, Justin and Tommy will represent us in the skills competition.

It's also time to resolve the Andrew issue. I haven't heard from father or son since the Gretzky but I know there's some level of expectation that Andrew will play goal again. I send an e-mail to his dad. Trying to be tactful, I suggest Andrew hasn't been too enthusiastic lately, and ask if he still has goalie aspirations. Forty-five minutes later, my phone rings. It's his dad.

Our conversation lasts over an hour. Though civil, Andrew's father makes it clear this has not been the experience he signed up for. He wishes he'd pulled Andrew off the team at the beginning of the season and put him where he could play goalie full time. If he were playing every game, he has no doubt Andrew would be much better. Playing net is what Andrew lives for and to his eyes, Andrew has the talent. He wants Andrew to play at least one more game in net.

I let the other coaches know what's happened. Their reply is equally quick. Andrew has had enough chances to prove himself. He doesn't try hard in practices or games. It's not fair to the team. They'll support whatever decision I make, but no one wants to see Andrew in net again.

The best solution would be for Andrew's mom to step in. She once told my wife how delusional Andrew is. "He's so funny," she said. "He actually thinks the team will suffer if he's not there." Then she burst out laughing. Why couldn't the acorn fall closer to the mother's tree?

I call his dad back and tell him Andrew can play net in our Wednesday practices (since we need two goalies), but as for the games, including our February tournament, we'll go with Tommy. The dad's not happy but says okay. Thanks to George, I'm able to give him the name of an instructor who lets goalies play for free every Saturday night. Andrew's dad says he'll follow up and hopes that will give his son the goalie time he wants.

Our final league game is against the Huskies, the league's most improved team. We have a full lineup and the sicklies have improved, but we're still not one hundred percent. Further, a win or loss makes no difference to us, or the Huskies, in terms of final standings. The game is predictably dull until one play suddenly turns the contest into an enduring memory for two parents and one set of coaches. Midway through the second period, Braeden picks up the puck behind his net. The kid who couldn't skate, at least according to his dad, heads up ice. He dekes out one opponent, then another and glances at the bench.

"Keep going," yells Brad.

"All the way Braeden," I shout.

On he goes. A third, fourth and fifth Huskie are unable to stop him. He shoots. Their goalie makes the save and the game ends in a two-two draw; but all any of us can talk about afterwards, is Braeden's coast-to-coast, Bobby Orr-style rush.

The standings are confirmed. We do indeed finish first. Our margin over the Giants is two points—had Tommy not tilted his head just enough, the order would be reversed. It gives us a good excuse to cheer louder than ever at game's end, but coming a week late, it's kind of anticlimactic. We'll get our trophies at the League Championship Game, when they present all the awards.

The season stats are finalized and ours are impressive. On average, we scored just under four and a half goals a game and gave up two and a half. Five of the top ten scorers are Cougars with Mike leading everyone by six points. There are seven players who were awarded ten or more assists—five are Cougars. Our team scored more goals than anyone else, finishing with eighty-eight. Second highest was sixty-five. Team assists were 120—almost double the next highest total. That's the stat I'm happiest with, and the one that doesn't surprise me. It would be impossible to watch any of our games and not notice we pass into the slot more than any other team by a huge margin.

Still, that was the past and the playoffs are looming. With two ties to end the season and half the team recovering from illness, we need this tournament. We're guaranteed three games in two days against good competition. It allows me to tweak the lines, something I've been toying with for the past month. I've always thought Ryan and Mike would play well together, but Mike and Turner worked so well for so long, I couldn't break them up. This tournament gives me a chance to try it in games that don't impact the league standings.

Our first game is on Olympic-sized ice—approximately the same length as our regular ice but almost twenty feet wider. My first thought, ironically, is how much of an advantage it will give us. We've become a skating and passing team—the extra room should give us a leg up on anyone. For the last few weeks we've practised bringing the puck into the other team's end along the boards, trying to draw the defence wide so we can pass the puck back to the third forward, hopefully alone, in front of the net. This rink will provide the ideal venue to bring the point home.

The strategy works. We dominate the game, get numerous breakaways and all three lines score. The four-two final flatters our opponents.

For lunch we head to the local roadhouse. On the ride over, Will, Joel and Travis join us in the van. Mike asks me to put *Queen's Greatest Hits* in the tape deck and fast-forward it to a certain well-known arena anthem. Minutes later, four eight-year-old boys are stomping their feet and clapping their hands in unison. In the rear view mirror, I can see Will and Joel with eyes closed, rocking their heads back and forth wildly. I can't help but laugh until suddenly I feel the van shaking.

"Guys, you're knocking us off the road."

I turn down the volume and the singing gives way to hysterical laughter. Fortunately for my shocks, we've pulled into the restaurant parking lot. The boys jump out and immediately tell their teammates how they made the coach's van rock and roll.

Our afternoon game is on a regular-sized rink but we do just as well. Our opponents score a late goal to make it a four-two final, but again, the score was closer than the play. By winning both our games, we know we'll finish first or second in our group and play in either the Championship or Consolation Final on Sunday. Coincidentally, it's the same day the Canadian men's team plays for Olympic gold.

Our last game of the round robin is Saturday morning in an arena with seating for a thousand. It looks to have been built in the sixties, and with its dressing rooms wedged under the stands, does have some character.

"This team sounds pretty good," says Justin's father. "They haven't lost a game all season."

They're called the Tigers. Walking around I'd noticed the matching jerseys, jackets and hockey bags. They play in the same league as the teams we played yesterday, so being undefeated just means that they've beaten the same teams we have.

We're supposed to start at eleven o'clock but we're still waiting for the Zamboni at ten minutes after. A tournament organizer pulls me aside and says we'll have to start the game without a flood.

The Tigers are good but we score first. Mike picks the puck off a defenceman in front of their net and slides it by the goalie. Otherwise, the play is even. They're somewhat of a gritty team— solid defensively and aggressive with their sticks. With our mix of talent, we're like a counterpuncher, using speed and skill to take advantage of opportunities. When the period ends, we're still up one-nothing.

The same organizer calls the referees to the edge of the rink; then they skate to the benches and give us the bad news. Play will have to stop for ten minutes while the Zamboni floods the ice. I point out it's not needed and suggest they let us finish. The other coach agrees but it's not up to us. They want the ice flooded. They'll give us another warm-up once it's done.

Both teams sit on the bench, watching the Zamboni go round and round. I'm not happy with the delay. One team will be affected more than the other. It's the same for both but I know one will handle it better. It's always the case when something stupid happens. I just hope it's us who comes out on top.

We're off the bench for a quick skate before starting the second period. There's still water on the ice when play begins. The Tigers come out flying. We're hemmed in our own end for most of the opening minutes. They finally score on a complete fluke. One of their wingers centres the puck and it deflects off another forward's skate into our net.

"Hey, they kicked it in," protest two of our players straight away.

"No, it was an accident," I reply. "Unless they do it on purpose, it counts."

Thirty seconds later, they force a faceoff in our zone. They win the draw and pass it back to their defence for a shot. From the bench I can see the shot clearly. Unfortunately, I can also see Tommy is completely screened. He pokes his head one way, just as the puck arrives the other. It's two-one them.

Two minutes later, they make it three-one. I wish I could call a time out. We've stopped skating. We're not pursuing them nearly as hard as we did in the first.

"Okay guys, let's just take this shift by shift, okay?" I say on the bench. "Ryan, Mike, Will—all I want you to think about is this next shift. Go out there and pretend you're playing Raptors, okay? Let's get that puck."

The boys improve and we do get a shot, but it's a weak one. Still, it picks up our team and slowly we crawl back into the game. Just when the play seems to be even again, they get another break. Early in the third period, we're passing out of our zone when the puck hits the back of our player's skate. It deflects right to a Tiger who centres it. The kid we've been told is their best makes no mistake. It's four-one.

"That's it. That's the game," says George, disappointed. "We won't be in the championship now."

"Shift by shift guys, okay? Don't give up." I say the words but in my heart, I agree with George. I can't see us coming back against this team.

Fortunately, the boys aren't as convinced. Three minutes later, Mike intercepts a pass near centre and finishes off his breakaway with a wrist shot into the mesh. Then, with a little over two minutes left in the game, Joel takes a pass from Will and wrists it high past the goalie, stick side. It's four-three and our guys are suddenly much more animated. Justin's line takes to the ice. They keep up the pressure but can't get a shot. With a minute and a half left, we get a faceoff in their zone—just what I wanted.

"Mike, Ryan—out you go. Travis, Joel, you too. Justin, stay out there. Play behind Mike—you'll be our second centre. Robert, you play defence and cover for the others, okay? You'll be the only guy back—play in the middle. Now everybody," I say, looking directly into their eyes. "Go for the net. We need a goal."

Brad calls Tommy to the bench. Our net is empty. George's eyes widen. I know he's consistently told everyone I'm the fairest coach he's ever seen. I wonder what he thinks of me stacking this line. I don't see a choice. The Tigers are Select. They've stacked their team.

The crowd is noticeably louder as the puck drops. No player is able to hang on to it for long since all are desperate. A Tiger fires it into our zone, well wide of the net. Fortunately, Travis is back to cover and clears it up the boards. Mike gathers it near centre. I look across the ice. The only one with him is Ryan. For some reason everyone else is hanging back.

"You've got Ryan with you!" I scream, but there's no possible way Mike can hear me with the crowd roaring.

Then he glances to the right side of the rink. He sees Ryan. But instead of passing, he takes off up the boards. There's hardly any room and it looks like the defenceman has him. Mike flips the puck over his stick and squeezes through. I can't believe it. There's only one Tiger between Mike and the goalie. Mike's flying but the guy has the angle. Carrying the puck far in front of his body near the boards, Mike gets around him but he's run out of rink. Finally, he passes toward Ryan. The puck slides across the ice, headed for the top of the crease, the same spot Ryan's racing to. The Tigers' top player, chasing the play dives, his stick stretched far in front of him. He blocks the pass, then follows the puck and crashes into the boards. The buzzer sounds. We've lost.

"You had to do it, didn't you?" screams George as Mike and

the others arrive at the bench. "Had to be the hero. Couldn't let someone else, could you?"

At first I think he's kidding. George does have a strange sense of humour. But then he looks at me and says: "Why didn't he pass sooner? We could've tied it up."

"George, that's what we've been teaching them," I say calmly. "Take the puck in wide, pass it out front."

"Yeah, but . . . ah forget it." He turns and visibly upset, gathers the spare sticks the boys had brought to the bench. Brad's quiet, non-committal. I can't tell if he agrees with George or not.

None of us speak to each other on the way back to the dressing room. After I lead the boys in our usual three cheers, I go for a walk. George and I have been through a lot together, mostly in soccer. How can he scream at a kid, any kid, let alone mine? Reviewing the play doesn't help. Why did everyone hang back, including Joel? It's too bad but, in the circumstances, I don't see how it could have turned out differently.

When I return to the dressing room, all seem to be in good spirits. A few parents have gained some satisfaction in how uneasy the Tigers' parents were. "That's the first time they've really been challenged," says Justin's dad, chuckling. "You should've seen them. They were going bananas."

As I suspected, George meets me in the parking lot, all smiles. He asks for confirmation of our next game and offers to buy me a coffee or something. It's his way of apologizing. There'll be no mention of the game or how it ended. I picked George as an assistant because his heart's in the right place. It is, but like many others, including me, hockey can get the better of your emotions from time to time. I know I wanted to win that game. Take away the first half of the second period, and it might've been our best hockey of the season.

For his part, Mike's completely oblivious to the whole incident. On the drive home, I explain what happened to my wife, but Mike claims he didn't know George said anything to him.

The Consolation Final is set for ten o'clock Sunday morning. Arriving at the arena, it's quickly apparent the word got out on how close we came to beating the Tigers. We're playing another team from their league, the Outlaws, currently in second place. On my way to the dressing room, I overhear two different conversations mentioning our game yesterday. Neither one involves parents I recognize.

When I'm handed the game sheet a couple of things strike me. The Outlaws have their lineup preprinted on stickers. It saves the coach having to write the names on the game sheet by hand. It's common for Select teams. Their coaching staff, however, is not. First, there's no less than five, and second, not one of them has a son on the team. None of these teams pay their coaches. Why would five adults come out to so many games and practices for a bunch of eight-year-olds they don't even know? They must be retired.

When the teams take the ice, Brad, George and I head for the far bench. The other coaches arrive late and they're all in their thirties or forties—definitely not retired.

Once the puck drops, we start quickly. For the first two and a half minutes, the puck stays in their end. When they finally get it out, they weave into our zone and score on their first shot. Two minutes later, it's two-nothing. We've had five more shots and Tommy's been in position. Either they're lucky or extremely well coached since both shots have been perfect.

"Don't worry guys," I say after the second goal, "we're all over these guys. They can't hold us off forever."

We continue to dominate the play but it isn't until the final minute of the period that we finally break through. Mike completes a neat three-way passing play with Ryan and Will to make it two-one heading into the second.

"They've shortened the bench, eh?" Brad says between shifts.

"What—already?"

"He's only going with two lines. Five kids in the middle of the bench haven't been on yet."

I shake my head. "Well, you've got to admit, this is a pretty big game," I add, widening my eyes. "A Consolation Final."

Brad laughs.

Like most of our games, the referees aren't calling any penalties. But this one's getting chippier. At first, it was just the odd slash or hook, but in the second period they're getting more flagrant. Kevin takes a cross-check in the back when he's leaving their zone. Turner gets elbowed. Ryan is slashed well after he's passed the puck.

"Hey ref, you might want to watch behind the play," I say as he skates by. "There's been a few fouls back there." I try not to sound critical, since sometimes it'll backfire. He doesn't respond but I'm sure he's heard me.

The fouls continue and then one too harsh to ignore. Joel passes the puck behind our net and up the boards. As he watches the pass, an Outlaw player skates behind him and slashes his legs out from under him, sending Joel sprawling into the back of the net. The referee stands in a straight line between Joel and me. He's looking right at it. He doesn't raise his arm, but continues to look at Joel. Joel is lying on the ice, behind the net. Finally the referee blows his whistle.

Brad rushes out to see how Joel is. In the meantime I signal the ref over.

"What's the call?" I ask, trying to remain calm.

"I had to stop the play. He's injured."

"Yeah but what's the call. What penalty are you giving them?"

"There's no penalty."

"Aw, come on. You were looking right at it. How could you not call that? He took his legs out. The puck was nowhere near them."

The ref turns and skates away.

"You got to be kidding!" I yell after him. "I know you saw that. I was looking right at you. You definitely saw it. How can you not call a penalty!"

The two refs huddle together on the far side of the ice, talking. Meanwhile, Joel gets up and Brad brings him to the bench.

"You okay Joel?" I ask.

"He slashed me from behind. For no reason."

"I know. The ref saw it too. I can't believe he didn't call it."

Play continues and so do the non-calls. Ryan carries the puck up the right side of the ice, an Outlaw hooking at him from behind. Mike catches up, heading for the net. At the blue line, another Outlaw grabs Mike's stick and lifts it up in the air.

"Interference!" I yell. "Call the interference!"

Ryan takes the puck to the hash marks and centres it, but Mike's stick is still being held high in the air, a good three feet off the ice. The puck slides past, into the opposite corner. Finally the Outlaws' player releases Mike's stick.

"I don't believe this." I glance at Brad who raises his eyebrows. "What is going on out there?"

Will comes off crying. He says he got kicked in the back of the leg. Next shift Justin complains one of their players slashed his arm where there's no padding. Two minutes later, Ryan's wincing. He says he got speared in the stomach.

The ref skates to a stop in front of our bench, watching as the play continues. I take up a spot directly behind him, moving one of our players to make room. "I don't know Turner," I say. "I have no idea why the refs won't call the penalties."

Turner looks up as if to ask: Are you talking to me?

"I know he's looking right at them," I continue. "He sees the slashes, the trips. He saw Joel thrown into the net. But he won't make the call. I don't know what's going on." The back of the ref's helmet is no more than twelve inches from me and I'm speaking directly toward his ear. He doesn't so much as flinch.

But as luck would have it, an Outlaw slashes Travis' arm right in front of us. "See. That was clearly a slash and he's looking right at it. But he's not going to call it. Don't ask me what's going on."

The play moves to the other end and the ref skates away. I know he heard me. But he didn't so much as glance my way.

The infractions continue. Joel goes down again. A minute later, it's Mike's turn to come off crying.

"First he whammed me with his elbow, then he punched me in the throat."

I have no idea what to say. At least four kids are watching me, as if I have the answer that will make it right. "Well . . ." I'm trying hard to think of something. Finally the words come out. "Hit him back."

Mike instantly stops crying. Turner looks at me as though he's wondering if he actually heard what he thought he heard. No one says anything more.

"I probably shouldn't have said that," I whisper to Brad. "But I don't know what to do. These refs aren't calling anything."

"No, you're right. There comes a point where you have to look after yourself."

With all the chippiness, the game isn't much of a game anymore. They add two goals in the second, one off a goalmouth scramble, the other off a turnover in our end. But rather than watch the play, I'm focused on the refs. And with each missed call, I let them know I saw the infraction. "What about the slash? Going to call that?" "Hooking—you're allowed to hook in this town, are you ref?"

A little over halfway through the third, Turner watches an Outlaw skating toward our net. He puts his stick in the boy's skate blade and lifts the kid's feet off the ice. It's a deliberate, blatant trip. The ref instantly raises his hand for the first penalty of the game.

I wait until the arena is quiet. "What's the call, ref?" I shout.

"Tripping," he yells back.

"Yeah? Well the big question is: how would you know, huh? The way this game's been going, I thought you didn't know what a trip was. How come you know now, huh?"

"Good one coach," says Joel, sitting beneath me.

I didn't think I could feel this exasperated. My hands are literally shaking. There's a hollow feeling in the pit of my stomach. They score on the power play, but then Mike sets up Will right off the ensuing faceoff to make the final five-two. As the buzzer sounds, an Outlaw swings his stick at Joel and Joel goes after him. The ref intervenes, treating Joel as if he were the offender.

"What are you yelling at him for?" shouts George. "The other guy started it."

The ref waves his hand at George as if to blow him off. The tournament organizer rushes up to me and asks if I've picked an MVP for the Outlaws.

"Yeah—the ref," I answer without hesitation.

The organizer laughs politely. It's strange though—I get the sense he agrees with me. "Why don't I let their coach pick a player," he says.

"Good idea."

There's a brief trophy presentation on the ice. Neither the players nor coaches shake hands. They didn't come looking for us and I didn't go looking for them. This is the first time I've ever lost a game and not shaken the other coach's hand but I don't care. Kids aren't that dirty unless someone tells them it's alright.

Once the last trophy's handed out, we quickly head for the dressing room. All the talk is about the refs and what cheaters the Outlaws are. Ryan's dad pulls me aside.

"You might want to know this," he says. "They stacked their team."

"What do you mean?"

"Braeden's mom knows someone whose son plays on another

team—the Jaguars. They're in this tournament but on the other side of the draw. She saw them and asked what they were doing here. They said today, they're playing for the Outlaws. Apparently there were four of them. Are they allowed to do that?"

"No. You can only use players registered on your team. That's why they get everyone to sign in."

"Well, you might want to talk to her because they definitely used players from the Jaguars."

I leave the dressing room and the first person I run in to is Braeden's mom. She repeats the story, adding that the woman she knows is a good friend of hers and it's definitely true—four Jaguars played for the Outlaws.

This is like a nightmare that won't end. How can a grown man tell four kids to play for another team? And what did he tell the kids he replaced? Stay home today? They'd have to switch socks, jerseys, maybe even pants to make it work. For what? A consolation trophy!

"Would Braeden's mom tell the tournament organizer what happened?" asks Brad when I give him the news.

"I don't know. It'd be putting her on the spot. She might get her friend in trouble."

"T.J., you can't say anything unless you can prove it."

"Yeah I know. It's funny, though. I wouldn't be surprised if the tournament guys already know. They're local teams. We're not. Maybe they told them they could."

"No. That's pretty sleazy."

"It's Select. They get to pick the best kids anyway."

"Kids' hockey," replies Brad, shaking his head. "Unbelievable."

I decide it's pointless to raise it. I don't want to put Braeden's mom up to it, and I think the odds are pretty good the organizers wouldn't care. Besides, what are they going to do? Replay the game? Give us the consolation trophies instead? We're not coming back for another game and their trophies don't look any different than ours. Morally, I'd like to take them to task, but practically, I can't see any upside. If the coaches are the type of men who'd do this to kids, exposing it isn't going to change anything. And if the coach says he cleared it with the organizer, then what? All the organizer would say is, it's a Select tournament—you can pick who you want. In the end, the only people who'd feel strange about it would be Braeden's mom and her friend. It's just something else to make me angry.

We pile in the van and head home. At three o'clock, Mike and I return for the all-star game. As we walk into the arena, the atmosphere has turned very chummy. The same refs I was yelling at earlier are laughing and chuckling with coaches I recognize from this morning. Our eyes connect and they immediately stop smiling. Then they look away.

Mike picked number nine for his all-star jersey. It's red with a maple leaf on the chest—perfect for Olympic Sunday. Across the leaf it reads *All-stars*. We paid the fifty dollars so his name appears in big block letters across the back—his very own all-star jersey.

A coach arrives and asks if I'd like to help out on the bench. He's extremely friendly and we share a few laughs about hockey and kids. Before we take to the ice, the word gets out—Canada is leading midway through the third.

I've brought my camera to take shots of Mike and Travis before the game. I've told the coach I'll work the door but I'll also be taking lots of pictures. As it turns out, the game isn't great. One of the teams is short a few players. Mike scores the first goal from behind the net. It's a fluke but it proves to be the winner in a twelve-nothing rout. Travis plays great; skating and passing as well as I've ever seen him. It's too bad Dave's on a plane out west. He would've enjoyed seeing Travis play like this.

Early in the second, between shifts, an announcement comes over the speakers "Attention, ladies and gentlemen. For those of you interested in another game being played today, Canada has just won the gold medal. I repeat, Canada wins gold." Instantly the crowd roars and the kids bang their sticks on the ice.

Mike's quiet on the drive home. It gives me a chance to think about the day. I've changed my mind about the opposing coaches. Although the four subs might have replaced injured or sick players, there's also a good chance the Outlaws' coaches told four eight-year-olds to stay home. Someone should stick up for those kids. I decide to write an e-mail to the tournament organizer when I get home.

As for the referees, this was the first time I've ever let myself get so carried away. Now I wonder why. In recorded history, no one's ever changed a call because a coach disagreed. The more I think about it, the clearer it becomes. Referees are a distraction. They can't help you with the task at hand. Whether they make every call, no call or completely biased calls, it makes no difference. You still have to clear the puck from your own end, work it up the ice and get the puck in front of the other team's net. Talking, yelling or gesturing at them can only distract you.

I'm the coach, the guy who's supposed to set the example. I can't let myself be distracted like that again.

As a final postscript, I sent the e-mail and even a reminder. No reply.

THE PLAYOFFS

"Okay guys," starts Dennis, "I called this meeting to go over the rules for the playoffs."

The coaches gather between two of the rinks at IceTime. Everyone goes quiet.

Dennis explains how the playoffs are a new season with everyone starting from scratch. We'll be divided into two groups of four teams, based on the final standings. As the first place finishers, we're in Group A with the fourth, fifth and eighth place teams—the Wildcats, Hawks and Falcons respectively. Over the next month, we'll play each of them as well as two teams from Group B. The winner of Group A plays the winner of Group B for the championship. Everything he says is written on the schedule produced at the beginning of the year, so it's hardly surprising.

"Now, let's make sure we understand the rules for who finishes first in each group, particularly when teams are tied." These also appear on our schedule. The first test is most points, based on two points for a win and one for a tie. If the teams have the same number of points, it goes to most wins, then goal differential, then goals for, goals against, and finally a playoff game if necessary. Of the four coaches from last year only one is listening. It's old hat to the rest and they're whispering about something else. One of the new coaches asks for clarification.

"Basically, to clinch it, you have to beat every team in your group, plus one," I interject, recalling the rule from last year.

"That's right," replies Dennis.

"So if I win four games but lose to someone in my own group, and they win four games, I'm out, right?"

"Depends who they lost to," says another.

"No—they beat the team they're tied with," protests a third.

"It still depends."

"Hang on, hang on," says Dennis, with an air of finality. He opens a folder he's been carrying and pulls out a copy of the schedule. As he reads the black and white, he goes through it for everyone. "Okay, first test is points—they'd both have eight so they're tied on points; next is wins—they'd each have four so they're still tied; then comes goal differential. So it depends on what the scores of the games were."

"There's no head-to-head?" I ask. I'm surprised. Last year the head-to-head was one of the first tests—if you beat the team you were tied with, you got through, regardless of what the scores of the other games were. I know because that's how Joe's team made it to the championship.

Dennis doubles checks the schedule. "Nope. No head-to-head," he confirms.

"That's not the way it used to be," replies another coach, equally surprised.

"I know. But that's what it says. I guess they changed it."

"Wow," I say. "That's a pretty big change. It definitely takes the pressure off." The head-to-head provision creates games you must win—those against the teams in your own group. Lose one and you no longer control your destiny. With no head-to-head, you can lose to anyone and still get into the championship game.

Walking back to our dressing room, I'm happy. This is good for us. Although the schedule is designed to favour the first place team—we play eighth, seventh, sixth, fifth and fourth in that order—it could easily work against us. With the exception of the Pythons, none of these teams have given us much competition. Overconfidence might cause us to lose one of those games. However, with no head-to-head, we'd have to lose two to be out of it. I can't see that happening, not the way we're playing.

Our first match is against the Falcons, the eighth place finisher. We played them twice during the season, winning six-three and seven-one. The kids remember our lopsided win, but it doesn't affect them. Nearly the entire game is played in the Falcons' end of the rink. Their goalie is outstanding. At the end of the first period, it's still scoreless. "Don't worry boys," I say. "We're all over them. They can't hold us off forever." It wasn't a difficult prediction. However, the three-one final is a testament to how well that young goalie played. Our forwards attacked the Falcons' zone relentlessly, usually getting two or three shots a shift. All three lines scored but they had to work for it.

The Sharks are up next, and they too have an outstanding goalie. But playing one good netminder has focused our kids, particularly the forwards. We're not missing a beat in games or practices. Once again, all three lines score in a five-nothing romp.

The Pythons finished sixth and gave us trouble in spots. We split our season series and they have a lot of individual talent— the league's second highest goal scorer for one. I was surprised they didn't finish higher and sure enough, as the first period ends, they're up one-nothing. But like our earlier games, it's clear which group of boys form the superior team. We pass better, and in this game are more determined. For the third game in a row, all three lines score. The final is five-one in our favour. Mike collects a hat trick to become the leading scorer in the playoffs.

Our fourth game is a rematch I've worried about since the buzzer ended our last meeting. The Hawks are a much better team than they showed in the fourteen-two drubbing we gave them in January. I was hoping to avoid them in the playoffs, but they ended up fifth so they're in our group. In the playoffs, they've won two of three. The Wildcats have a win, a tie and a loss. So we lead the group with six points; the Hawks are second at four.

Given the issues we've had all season in determining the correct standings, I've kept a record of the scores from all games. Our cumulative goals for and against is thirteen-two, giving us a goal differential of plus eleven. It only takes a few minutes to calculate the same stat for everyone in our group. The Hawks are second at plus three. So we're two ahead in points and eight ahead in goal differential. We're definitely in good shape.

At practice, several of the parents want to know how close we are to clinching. I review the group standings and explain how the tiebreaker works.

"So as long as we win one more game, and stay close in the other, we're in," says Justin's dad.

"That's right," I assure him, feeling pretty happy with the situation myself.

"There's no way we're going to lose two in a row," adds Braeden's father. "I don't want to jinx us but I can't see that happening."

"Me neither, but it's the playoffs, you never know." I don't believe anything can stop us now, but like Braeden's dad, I don't want to say too much out loud. Everything's going great. No sense tempting the hockey gods.

"Let me tell you something," I say to the boys in the pre-game talk Saturday morning. "The Hawks have been dying to play us ever since that last game. They don't care if they beat any other team this year, they don't care if they make it to the championship or not. They want one thing and only one thing—to beat the Cougars."

The guys are listening as calmly and patiently as ever.

"If we win this game, do we get to play in the championship?" asks Braeden.

"I think so, but just worry about the game, okay? Worry about playing your position and doing the things we always do. Let's go out and play like raptors, okay?"

Fifteen seconds in, Travis take a pass from Joel and makes it look like this could be a repeat of our last contest, wristing it high into the mesh. But twenty seconds later, the Hawks have tied it up. The game is fast; the puck moves from one end to the other. Two minutes later, on his first shift, Mike takes a pass from Turner at centre. He dekes out everyone including the goalie, to make it two-one us. But the Hawks won't get left behind. Just a minute and a half later, they pull even again on a nice passing play.

The second period starts the same way, only in reverse. The Hawks pot one forty seconds in, only to have Turner tie it up twenty-five seconds later from Mike and Will. The goalies aren't playing badly, but rather, the shots taken are all labelled. The next one however, isn't. Mike's unable to get off the ice to end his shift and ends up staying out for almost three minutes. He has good endurance but he's clearly spent. He's heading for the front of our net when the Hawks centre the puck. Mike arrives and instinctively moves his stick to stop it. Unfortunately, he ends up redirecting the puck into our net. There were no Hawks close to him. From the bench you can see the look in Tommy's eyes as he glances at Mike, saying, what have you done? Mike skates solemnly to the bench.

"It's okay Mike," says Brad when he arrives. "It's happened to all of us. Don't worry about it."

Mike looks up at me as he walks by. His eyes confirm what I suspected: absolutely no one in this arena feels worse than Mike.

"You know you did the right thing," I say, referring to his attempt to intercept a centreing pass. "It was just bad luck. We'll get it back. Okay? Think about scoring."

Mike turns to watch the play. His next couple of shifts are solid, but he can't manage to score. It looks like they're keying on him, but he's playing well. I don't think it'll matter. As a team we're still okay, although we don't seem quite as sharp as we have been. The second period ends four-three them.

The Hawks start the third the same way they've started every period today, with a goal in the first forty seconds. One of their speedier players picks up a pass at centre and takes it all the way. They lead five-three. Two minutes later, Mike's made it a one-goal game again. They definitely are keying on him but he's playing determined hockey. I have him back with Turner and the two of them, in tandem with Will, are pressuring the Hawks every time they're out there. With over seven minutes left, they look like they'll score at least one more today.

While play continues, I think about playoff standings. If we lose by one goal, we're tied with the Hawks on points and wins, but six ahead on goal differential. That means if we win our next game by one goal, they'd have to win theirs by seven to catch us. I can't see that happening. On the other hand, if we lose by two goals, our lead in goal differential shrinks to four. It's still a stretch but obviously, it would be better to keep our goal differential where it is. When I look up at the clock and see five minutes remaining, I've already decided I'm not going to pull our goalie for an extra attacker. To finish ahead of us, the Hawks have to score seven more goals than we do. Scoring on an empty net is a lot easier than scoring on a goalie. I'll leave Tommy where he is.

Mike, Turner and Will take the ice for their last shift with two and a half minutes left. They're all over the Hawks. The puck stays in the Hawks end but their players are crowding the front of the net, sensing victory. With a minute and a half left, we change lines. We're still down a goal.

Travis stops on his way out and returns to the bench. "Do we need to score?"

"You should try your hardest to score Travis. We want to tie it up, for sure."

"Yeah but do we need to?" he asks, accenting the words *need to*. "To get to the championship?"

I'm not going to lie but I'm not going to give him an excuse to go easy either. "Travis, there's a minute and a half left. We're losing. Try your absolute hardest to get that goal, okay. Let's at least get a tie."

Travis skates to their zone for the faceoff. I've already explained the situation to Brad and George. They concur with my decision not to pull the goalie. Braeden, however, isn't so sure.

"Aren't we pulling the goalie?" he asks.

"No. I don't want to give them any easy goals. We're way ahead of these guys in goals so I don't want to let them get any closer."

He nods but I doubt he understands. For the next minute, we keep the play in the Hawks end. We're getting shots but no goal. With thirty seconds left, there doesn't seem to be much risk of an empty netter. "Should we pull him anyway?" I ask Brad.

"I would."

We signal Tommy to the bench and with Mike just off, I send Justin out as an extra attacker. I do it intentionally. Mike's bailed this team out many times before, but the team's playing better now and all three lines are scoring. I want to give someone else the chance.

Within ten seconds of pulling Tommy, a Hawk clears the puck and it's headed for our zone. The fastest Hawk is all over it and fires toward our net. The puck hits the boards behind. We get to it first, but they're pressuring us, keeping the puck in our end. The buzzer sounds. A one-goal loss.

In the dressing room after, parents and players all have the same question so I ask for quiet to let everyone know where we stand. "We're still first in our group, but now we have to win next week," I continue, emphasizing there's a second condition, "And we have to beat the Wildcats by as many goals as possible. We're six ahead on goal differential. So if we beat the Wildcats by one, the Hawks have to beat the Falcons by seven; if we win by three, they have to win by nine. And so on. The more we win by, the better it is."

"We're going to beat those guys fourteen-two," shouts Braeden.

"Well if we do, we'll get in for sure."

Speaking to parents individually as the boys get changed, they all seem to agree we're in good shape. Everyone thought we'd win today, but no one leaves worried.

On my way to the van, I run in to the Hawks coach and we chat briefly. Rose, our original convenor, arrives and congratulates me on finishing first. Then she turns to the Hawks coach and tells him how well his team played today. "So now you're in the driver's seat for the championship," she says.

"Yeah but anything can happen," he replies.

"Actually," I interject, "we're still first in the group. We're way ahead on goal differential."

"Yes but he's won the head-to-head," says Rose.

"There's no head-to-head this year."

"Yes there is. If two teams are tied, the first test is the head-to-head game."

"No, there isn't," I insist. "The tiebreak rules are right on the schedule. First is points, then wins, then goal differential. There's no head-to-head."

"I agree it's printed that way but it's a mistake. They found it a week ago. Dennis was supposed to tell you. The schedule is wrong. There's supposed to be a head-to-head test right after most wins."

A sinking feeling begins to form in my stomach. "Rose," I say, looking directly into her eyes the same way she did to me at the very start of the season, "that's not fair."

She pauses, a bit taken aback. "Well, I don't see why not. You're not going to tell me you were trying to lose."

"No. But I left my goalie in because we were so far ahead on goal differential. I didn't want to give them any easy goals. Don't forget, any goal they score affects the goal differential by two— theirs goes up and ours goes down. So yes, I was telling our guys to try and score, but I told them the most important thing was not to let the Hawks get any more goals."

This causes her to stop and think. She looks away. From the way she raises an eyebrow and takes a deep breath, it appears she sees how the rule could cause me to do that.

"But Rose," I continue, "how can you change the rules after the fact?"

"We're not changing the rules. That's the way it's always been. It was that way last year, the year before."

"Yeah, I know. I was the guy who brought it up with Dennis. He checked it out and said they changed it. He told me there was definitely no head-to-head."

"Well, you can take it up with the VP House League but I don't think it's going to help you. The truth is you lost the game."

"Yeah but there's a huge difference between thinking you're still in the lead, even if you lose, and thinking you have to score or you're out. Here I am, telling my guys to make sure the Hawks don't score and now you're saying, I should've been pulling out all the stops to get a goal ourselves."

"Okay, tell you what. I'll explain the situation to the VP House League Monday night. He may agree with you, but I doubt it."

Saying she's had more than enough hockey for one day, she excuses herself and leaves. The Hawks' coach is still standing beside me. "I didn't know there was anything written on the schedule," he says. "I just assumed it was head-to-head."

"It's not there. I asked Dennis all about it. I can't believe this."

"But T.J., you did pull your goalie."

"Yeah. When I figured there was no chance for you guys to score. The stupid thing is we had a faceoff in your end with a minute and a half to go. One of the kids asked me to pull the goalie but I said no, we didn't need to. I told them we were still ahead of you in the standings."

He has enough class not to say any more. The part of me that isn't fuming is beginning to feel like a sore loser. I tell him I'd better let my team know what the truth is and head for the exit.

The fuming part of me wins over when I get into our van. "I can't believe this," I growl, slamming my fist into the steering wheel. "I've done every stupid thing they've asked me, read all their stupid little books, followed all their stupid little rules, which, as it turns out, makes me the only frigging person in the entire universe to actually do it. And now this? How can they do this!"

"Calm down. For all you know, she could be wrong," says my wife. "Wait till you talk to Dennis. He knows what he told you."

Dennis is away this weekend, working. Usually that means he won't be home till late Sunday night. I decide I'll draft an e-mail as soon as I get home, then let it sit till I've calmed down, like maybe a year from now. Then I'll reread it and make sure I didn't say anything stupid before I send it to him. But one thing's for sure—I'm not taking this sitting down. I asked them about the rule, challenged them on it and then changed my strategy based on what they told me. They can't change it now.

OH YES THEY CAN

There are bigger tragedies in life than an eight-year-old boys' hockey team getting aced out of its championship game. But this seems so morally wrong, I have trouble thinking of anything else, or even how anyone else might feel, including a certain young player and a certain goal.

Mike barely says a word on the drive home from the arena, only a couple of questions to clarify what the rule change will mean to our hopes for the championship. For the rest of the day, he's different—a bit quieter, his giggles shorter, broken off. He claims nothing is wrong. When I tuck him into bed, we're momentarily alone. He sits up, looking pretty sober, almost solemn, and sighs loudly.

"Still thinking about that goal?" I ask. It's the first time we've spoken about it all day.

"Yeah," he says with a frown.

Mike scored two goals and assisted on another but neither one of us needs to say which goal we're talking about. "It's happened to a lot of great players. Chris Pronger did it a few weeks ago. I'm sure Orr's done it. Gretzky probably. There was even that guy who scored when his net was empty. Can you imagine that? They pull the goalie and you put the puck in your own net."

He laughs but only half-heartedly. It's not working. I'm struggling to find anything that might help him. "Did I ever tell you about the one I scored?"

"You scored on your own net?"

"Uh-huh. A real beaut' too. It wasn't like yours. Mine was probably the best shot I ever took. I was playing defence, got the puck in my own zone, turned and fired. It was supposed to go behind the net and up the boards. Instead it was perfect—inside the far post, high on the stick side."

"What did they say to you?"

"Not much. The coach said it was a nice shot."

Mike laughs.

"Then he said, 'Too bad you weren't facing the other way.'"

He laughs again.

"It's funny though—none of my teammates said a thing. I guess they knew it was an accident. Besides, I was the best defenceman. The team would've been nowhere without me."

Mike seems to ponder this last thought.

"But man, you should've seen it. What a shot. One timer. Boom. Absolutely perfect. High in the mesh. The goalie never had a chance." With each phrase, Mike laughs a little more. "You know, it was probably the best goal I ever scored." That one cracks Mike up completely and he laughs hysterically. "Good night, bud," I say, kissing him, "see you in the morning."

Downstairs, I sit back in the recliner and try to watch the Leafs' game without thinking about my juniors.

"So," starts my wife, once she's back in the family room after her turn with the boys, "what's this I hear about you scoring on your own net? Sounded pretty funny."

I'm glad Mike's feeling better but I'm still on a slow burn over the rule change. My intention to wait twenty-four hours before sending a note to Dennis didn't last long. I arrived home from the arena at ten o'clock this morning, drafted the note, and as planned, set it aside. However, by noon, I'd edited it on three separate occasions and hit the send button. By three thirty, I'd thought of a few more things to say and sent a second. At quarter after four, after dreaming up yet another "one more thing," I sent my third, although on that one I apologized for clogging up his e-mail.

I couldn't believe how perfectly everything conspired against me. If they truly were going to change the rule, my hope lies in proving they'd told me differently and that my actions changed as a result. Although it was true, proving it seemed hopeless. When I challenged them on the rule in front of everyone, few were listening—only two of the coaches. Both have now been eliminated. Even if they did remember, why would they stand up for me? We've already won a trophy. No one wants to see us get two.

And the fact is I did pull the goalie. I know it was only because the kids were bugging me, but anyone watching the game would say I waited too long. They'd have no way of knowing the truth. To them, any complaints seem like sour grapes.

Then there was an e-mail I sent the team when the playoffs began. I wanted to keep everyone motivated throughout so, rather than explain the new tiebreaking rule, I simply said we had to win every game. Now I was saying we didn't and claimed they changed the rule. What will the parents think? The rookie coach hadn't read the rules, or if he did, didn't understand them. The stupid guy waited too long to pull his goalie. And when he did, he left the league's top scorer sitting on the bench.

No question—the circumstances make me look bad, including the e-mail I sent the team this afternoon informing them of this latest development. In it, I reproduced the tiebreaking rule, word for word, as it appeared on our schedule.

Playoff Tiebreaking Format
1. Most Points
2. Most Wins
3. Goal Differential
4. Most Goals
5. Fewest Goals
6. Playoff Game

Writing it out, I noticed the fifth test was also a mistake. No doubt they meant fewest goals against. I wondered if the league could somehow use that against me. Sorry guys—we made so many mistakes we're throwing the whole thing out.

Of course the most bothersome thing of all was the fact we lost. I knew the boys would have trouble getting up for this game. And the Hawks wouldn't. I still couldn't manage to overcome it. It ticked me off that while the Hawks were being told they had to win this game or they were out, I was telling our boys, it didn't matter as long as we're close. I wouldn't mind it so much if our best effort lost to their best effort, but this didn't feel like that at all. It felt like I'd been duped, made a coaching mistake and the team lost as a result.

Sunday morning brings plenty of e-mails from the parents but no response from Dennis. The parents are supportive and encourage me to take it up with the league if Dennis doesn't enforce the written rule. Ryan's dad brings up a point that could prove interesting. One of Ryan's friends plays for the Hawks. They noticed him at several positions throughout the game. Further, the coaches changed the order and composition of the lines to ensure their five best players were on the ice for the last two minutes. Both are clear violations of the league's playing rules. Ryan's dad would have no problem telling the convenor if required, adding those rules are black and white and haven't been changed.

Monday morning, at nine thirty, the phone rings. It's Dennis. Given the angst this has caused me, the conversation is surprisingly short. He doesn't see what the big deal is. The rule's in writing so the league will obviously follow it. He assures me Rose doesn't always know what she's talking about. As for the line juggling issue, he says the Hawks' coach has been accused of manipulating lines all season and been warned more than once. It's unfortunate but there's nothing anyone can do about it now. He'll talk to the VP House League tonight and call me tomorrow morning.

I'm relieved. I e-mail the team telling them it looks like we'll be okay—Dennis is on our side and knows the rule is in writing. However, when Ryan's dad hears they won't do anything about the line juggling, he's furious. "Why have the rule if they're not going to enforce it?"

I agree. It is ridiculous. All these rules are in writing but we have no idea what will or won't be applied. It's no better on the ice. The rules are clear but what the ref will call is anyone's guess.

On Tuesday morning my phone is silent. I send Dennis another e-mail, get no response, then call him at work mid-afternoon, apologizing for the interruption.

Again, the conversation is short. They're going to table the issue at a directors' meeting Wednesday night. It turns out we're not the only team impacted by this "mistake." The same rule was printed on all schedules for all divisions, so it's an issue everywhere. They want to hear what the directors say. He'll let me know Thursday morning.

I ask him for the flavour of the conversation and he suddenly gets a little uneasy. "They think there should be a head-to-head," he says.

"Me too," I reply quickly, "but that's not the issue. They had a rule they started the playoffs with and the coaches relied on it. They can't change it now."

"Yeah I know."

It's obvious Dennis will go with whatever the league decides. He claims he understands my point of view and how our actions changed, but I don't get the sense he'll be banging any tables at the directors meeting. Still, I know there are professionals on the board. Surely someone will realize a written rule can't be changed until the season is over.

After hanging up, I return to the computer. My days are supposed to be filled with writing—the other thing I took the year off work for. I've been trying to finish a science fiction novel, something I made notes on for years. But it's hard to concentrate. Then it hits me: my novel doesn't have anywhere near the ups and downs this kids' hockey season has. The truth I'm living is far stranger than the fiction I'm creating.

I let the parents know it will be Thursday before we hear. Some get restless. Justin's dad calls the Ontario Minor Hockey Association and speaks to the representative responsible for our town. The rep says he's been involved in hockey for thirty-five years and has never heard of a league not following a written rule. "Usually, the problem is they haven't written it down," he says. However, the OMHA has no jurisdiction over House League. He assures Justin's father the people in our town seem reasonable. He's sure it will work out fine.

What does the Green Book say? asks Kevin's dad, in another e-mail. *I know these people and it always comes down to the Green Book.*

The Green Book is the league's constitution, bylaws and playing rules. I copy out the relevant sections for him verbatim, complete with page numbers. The book separates the regular season and playoffs. The head-to-head test appears in the regular season part, but not the playoffs. In fact, the book states categorically the playoff rules may be different and will be communicated separately.

You've got a good point T.J., replies Kevin's dad. *I don't see how they can rule against you.*

Connor's dad practises law at a large firm in Toronto. He verifies the law does govern organizations like a minor hockey association. He says not following your own published rules is, in fact, illegal. However, fighting the issue through the courts would not be practical. It would take far too much time and cost too much money, given the issue at hand.

It occurs to me raising a lot of fuss over eight-year-olds playing hockey is ludicrous. I wonder if I should just back off and keep my mouth shut.

Images of the kids come to mind, how hard they try when they're on the ice. How often do I try that hard? Certainly in business there are plenty of times when I don't forecheck at all. Have I ever played like a raptor? Would the kids give up if they were in my shoes?

I picture Turner going to the net. One time he got knocked to the ice but kept his eyes focused on the puck. He still got the shot off.

"Hey, Coach," he said when he came to the bench, laughing. "I scored on my butt."

No. Fighting over kids' hockey doesn't make me feel like the most mature person on the planet, but giving up and walking away seems like a betrayal to the boys. They try their hardest. So should I. This isn't about winning or losing. The league made a rule. They wrote it down. I asked if they were sure. They said yes. I pointed out it was a big change from last year. They agreed. I relied on them. The team relied on them. Saying they're going to change it now, doesn't cut it. They're too late. They can't do it.

"How can they do that!" I blurt into the phone first thing Thursday morning.

"The board feels the tiebreaking rule as set out in the Green Book is the fairest way to handle the situation. The head-to-head test is in the Green Book. That's what we'll follow," replies Dennis.

"But it's not. The Green Book says those aren't the rules. Not for the playoffs."

"T.J., I'm just telling you what the board decided. They realize not everyone's going to be happy. It's unfortunate the mistake was made, but that's their decision. It's time to move on."

"What about the line juggling?"

"Don't even go there. It's your word against his."

"I've got a parent who'll confirm it."

"Doesn't matter."

"So I follow a rule that's in writing, and you say I shouldn't have because it was supposed to say something else. He violates a rule that's in writing, and you say you don't care. Bottom line: follow the rules, you lose, and break the rules, you win. Is that right?"

"I know it doesn't look good, but don't worry about it. Okay? For all you know, come Saturday, the Falcons will beat the Hawks, you'll beat the Wildcats, and then you're in."

Dennis is not the decision maker and I know he'd much rather see us in the final. So he's not the guy to argue with. I offer to replay the final five minutes, or even the entire game, but neither is accepted. Before hanging up, I warn him I'll have some angry parents on my hands. He says the board expects that.

By mid-morning, reactions are streaming in. Yesterday at practice, I taped a copy of the playing schedule to our dressing room door, highlighting in yellow the *PLAYOFF TIEBREAKING FORMAT*. Everyone knows this is not a rookie coach's mistake. This is a league that's decided, at its highest level, they're going to change a playoff rule, after virtually all the playoff games have been played. Although a few parents take it quietly, most are livid.

I write the VP House League and copy the team. I tell him the explanation we've been given, i.e. they're following the Green Book, doesn't make sense. I remind him of the rules that separate the playoffs from the regular season, as well as the Players Bill of

Rights which provides the *right to be treated fairly and with impartiality*, as well as the *right to participate in a program in which sportsmanship, honesty and integrity are the cornerstones*. Then I let all the parents know how they can get in touch with the VP House League.

Andrew's dad, on behalf of the sponsor, writes his own letter and gives it to me for proofreading. Worded nicely, it asks how a sponsor can support an organization that doesn't honour its own rules. He then hand delivers the letter to the VP House League's residence.

Tommy's mom and Braeden's dad, both send letters via e-mail. They're complimentary to me as a coach, and take the slant of asking how a parent can explain to their eight-year-old son the logic of changing a rule after the game has been played.

Other parents tell me they've called the league offices, but can't get through. Neither can I. Patrick's dad says his neighbour plays Peewee and was told there's no head-to-head this year. The best response of all comes from George who offers to do anything, "Even if I have to bite someone."

I visit the league offices but no one's there. It's during business hours but the premises are empty. There's not even a *Back in Five Minutes* sign on the door. It's starting to feel like we're barking at airplanes.

To make matters worse, on the home front, Mike complains he's not feeling well early Thursday night. He looks pale and has a slight fever. By midnight, he's emptied his stomach several times and is burning up. We tuck him into our bed, where we can monitor him throughout the night. On Friday morning, he's white as a ghost and his fever's raging. We keep him home from school. Thirty-six hours to our final playoff game, and as of now, Mike can't play.

By noon Friday, I'm still waiting for a response from the league. But now I'm wondering what I'm going to do if they just say no. I don't have any leverage. Say I refused to play our final game in protest. So what—they'll just say we forfeited and then we're out for sure. No, this isn't barking at airplanes; this is forechecking without a stick.

I have to re-focus the team. *Let's not forget,* I write in an e-mail, *we are still in this. Our goal at the beginning of the year was to teach these boys how to play hockey. We said we'd be the team that gets better and that's what we've been. Let's make Saturday's game our best of the season.*

Around ten thirty Friday night, an e-mail arrives from the VP House League. It's only a few lines long. He's reviewed the notes I've sent him as well as the notes from parents. He understands our frustration but believes the tiebreaking format as outlined in the Green Book is fairest to all. It was never their intent for any other format to be used in the playoffs. That's it.

So heading into the final playoff game, we're second in our group and no longer in control of our destiny. The game starts at five thirty tomorrow afternoon and right now, our leading scorer is too sick to play. Further, even if we win, the only way we can make it to the championship is if the Falcons, who finished last, can beat the Hawks, the team I've always thought had the most talent, and who I'm now told have consistently broken the rules to give themselves an even bigger advantage. There doesn't seem to be any chance our season won't come to a crashing end tomorrow night.

 A FITTING END

I'm not sure what to expect as I walk into IceTime for our final playoff game. There's been a lot of frustration expressed over the last few days. I wouldn't be surprised if it bubbles over in the dressing room. It's not something I want. We've worked hard and we are a good team. I really do want to go out on a high note.

They've put us in the farthest dressing room. I have to pass by a gathering of parents on the way. I overhear the Wildcats' coach explaining why they no longer have a chance to get into the championship. I hadn't realized but under the old rules, it was possible. With the new head-to-head test, they're out. Not surprisingly, the parents are upset. They're having the same reaction we did, but a few days later.

As usual, Ryan's already in the dressing room and getting ready as we enter. His dad looks at me and frowns, shaking his head, clearly disgusted.

"What can you say," I reply. "We still have a game, we're still in it. We've got to win."

"Yup, you're right," he says, still shaking his head. "But this town's the worst. Everything they do. Everything! I don't understand why they even have rules. Why put them in place if you're going to do whatever you feel like anyway?"

He's right and if this were a bar, I'd throw in my two, three and four cents worth. But it's not. In half an hour, sixteen kids are going to play what will probably be their last game of the season. I bite my tongue and just nod.

As the other parents file in, many express the same sentiment. But thankfully, it's all done quietly and quickly. Everyone knows the kids come first and there's nothing to be gained from dwelling on something that can't be changed.

Mike's feeling better. He started the day with six pancakes, thus passing the hunger test. His fever's gone and though he hasn't been moving much, he claims he's ready to go.

"No matter what happens," I start off, once the kids are dressed and the room has quieted, "tomorrow, each one of us gets a trophy. On the bottom of that trophy, it says *League Champions*."

Turner's eyebrows rise. Mike smiles. Tommy nods as if to say, only fair.

"All season long, we've been the team that gets better. Every game. Remember how we started. Some of your parents thought this would be a lousy team. I'll bet some of you did too."

Out of the corner of my eye I notice Justin's dad chuckling to himself.

"But we worked hard. We said we'd get better and we did. Think about some of the games we played: all-star teams, an undefeated Select team. We became so good, people had trouble believing we were house league."

Travis nods, a tinge of pride visible, even through his cage.

"Today's the last game of the playoffs. We're still the team that gets better. So guys, let's make this our best game of the season. Let's show everyone why that trophy says League Champions and why we won it. Alright?"

For once the boys let out a loud cheer and leap to their feet. They hurry out of the dressing room and onto the ice. The Wildcats are already out, skating their warm-up.

"As long as they play well, I don't care," I say to Brad on our way to the bench.

"I agree," he replies. "T.J., no matter what, it's been a great season. But don't give up yet. Stranger things have happened. We could get in."

Usually, on the weeks we play at IceTime, most of the parents stay in the restaurant where it's warm, but today, they're out and cheering as soon as we hit the ice.

The ref calls the teams to centre and drops the puck. The first period is slow. Passes just miss, shots are a foot or two wide. The teams are skating well but nothing much is connecting. The second period starts the same way but around the half way mark, it suddenly becomes a new game. One team's passes begin to connect. They look much sharper and soon are dominating the play. It's us. Over the final period and a half, we do in fact demonstrate why we're league champions. As one of the Wildcat parents would say after, the Cougars put on a clinic. Every line scores and every goal is at least a three-way passing play. The Wildcats barely touch the puck. Our defence gets the play going perfectly and the forwards anticipate their passes like we've only seen in practice. Late in the game, the best Wildcat slams his stick on the ice in open frustration. The final score is four-nothing. We've put together better games, but the last period and a half is our best hockey of the season. The team that said they'd get better, did.

As I walk to the dressing room I turn to George. "You know, we played great. I don't care. If that's how it ends, that's fine with me. What team in this league can play like that?"

George doesn't respond. He just nods. But I'm being honest. That was a great way to go out. The objective was to teach these boys how to play hockey. That game proved it. Mission accomplished.

The mood in the dressing room is jovial but not as celebratory as I thought it might be. Our three cheers are loud but the kids quickly get undressed. Every one of them wants to watch the Hawk game. It starts right after ours. The situation is now straightforward: if the Hawks win, they go to the championship, if they lose or tie, we do.

The entire team is soon in the corner bleachers, cheering loudly for the Falcons. Surprisingly, one of the loudest is Dave. I think it's the first time I've heard him all season.

The game will take about an hour to complete and I'm not anxious to subject myself to minute-by-minute anxiety. Between the four rinks and restaurant, there are always people I know, either on the ice or just hanging around. I spend most of the hour on a walkabout. My first stop is at a rink where the Giants are playing the Huskies. It's not a bad game but I've always had difficulty staying interested in other peoples' kids playing any sport.

I see a good friend of mine by the rink next door. Her daughter is about to play a game. I've coached the girl in soccer and always wondered what sort of hockey player she is. Unfortunately, after a few minutes' wait, we're told the other team didn't show up. The girls take to the ice but rather than scrimmaging, most of them start sliding along the ice on their bellies, seeing who can slide the furthest. My friend and I share a laugh over the difference between fourteen-year-old girls and boys, at least when it comes to a free sheet of ice.

I head upstairs to the restaurant. Braeden's mom is one of the first people to see me. "The Falcons are up one-nothing," she says excitedly.

I join the crowd by the windows. It's one of those ping-pong style games where each team fires the puck up the ice, not really looking for teammates. It could be like our game where play improves later on, but at this stage, they're not even trying to pass.

"I know I shouldn't take sides," says the Wildcats' coach, grabbing my arm in the crowd, "but I hope you guys make it. You're a much better team. It's not fair what they're doing with that rule. He told us there's no head-to-head. I saw you play the Hawks last week. I knew why you didn't pull your goalie. I thought it was the smart thing to do. I was surprised when you did."

"The kids were bugging me to," I reply, pleasantly surprised to find someone who actually thought I did the right thing. "But it taught me a lesson: no matter what—go for the win."

We chat a little more. Despite the fact we never ran any of our practices together, we both have a similar philosophy on how to handle kids and the way minor hockey teams should play.

It's not long before the Hawks tie it up, something I'm not surprised at. Justice will prevail, I think to myself, figuring the team with the most talent will win. There are plenty of upsets in sports, but in my coaching career, I've always been the victim of upsets, never the beneficiary. With the first period winding down, I resume my walkabout.

There's a men's game playing on the farthest rink and unlike many, this one's good enough to hold my attention. Momentarily. Ten minutes later I can't resist sneaking a look at the scoreboard down the hall. The Visitors are up two-one. I double-check to make sure the Falcons are sitting on the Visitors bench. They are. As I'm watching, a Hawk clearing shot caroms off the boards to another Hawk circling at centre ice, all alone. Even worse, two others join him—a three-on-none for half the ice. The Falcon goalie comes out to challenge. The Hawk shoots, but right into the chest protector. No rebound. It's still two-one.

It occurs to me the Hawks have to score two to put us out and the Falcon goalie is one of the league's best. But it's way too early to be thinking like that. I head back upstairs to find other parents I know from soccer and hockey. After as much small talk as I can muster, I'm back at the windows, this time for good, with seven minutes left in the game.

Our entire team is in the bleachers, and they're so loud, you can hear them through the glass. They not only cheer every Falcon who takes the puck off a Hawk, or clears the puck from their zone, they're also coaching the Falcon players, telling them to "shoot it up the boards," or "pass it out front," or "cover the man behind you." With the Hawk parents also in the crowd, it's a little embarrassing.

The first two scoring chances I see are both to the Hawks, but the Falcon goalie is equal to the task. His defence plays desperate, swarming the Hawk forwards whenever they're near the net. Then, after a couple of minutes in the neutral zone, the Falcons manufacture a chance of their own. As if responding to the kids in the crowd, they do in fact pass the puck out front. It's quickly slammed home to give them a two-goal lead.

"It looks like you're in," says the Wildcats coach, smiling broadly.

"Could be. You never know," I reply, not wanting to tempt the hockey gods.

"Oh come on," he says, "they're not going to score three goals in five minutes. Not on that goalie."

"Yeah, you're probably right. At least I hope so."

He laughs while a parent I know from another team taps me on the shoulder and congratulates me. Many of the Cougar parents see me and gather around.

"Can you believe it?" exclaims one, laughing, his eyes dancing.

"Isn't it great? They did it!" shrieks another.

"You see," says one mother calmly, "it all works out in the end. Justice is served."

It's funny—I feel more relief than excitement. For the past month I've considered the championship game as the fitting end to our season. Anything less was, to me, somewhat of a failure. We have worked harder than anyone else, and come farther. To not finish it off would have meant we'd faltered in the stretch. The way it unfolded, losing to a team we should have beaten, meant that not only had the players faltered, the coach had too. Now we're in and the world is feeling right again.

Amidst the handshakes and back slaps, I hear the buzzer sound and the roar from the bleachers. It occurs to me everyone will be leaving pretty quickly.

"Parents of the Cougars," I announce over the din of the crowd, "can we get together in the hallway for a minute? I want to have a quick word with the boys." It doesn't take long for the word to spread and we gather the team, away from the restaurant.

"Guys, listen up," I start. "Tomorrow afternoon we're going to be playing for the championship. Here's what's going to happen." I crouch to one knee. The boys sit around me, listening attentively. "First of all, there's going to be a big crowd. They invite all the teams and parents so there'll be a lot of people. Second, they're going to introduce every one of you before the game. They hand out the trophies afterward."

"Do we get two?"

"Yes. You'll get one for finishing first and another for being in the championship. It doesn't matter whether we win or lose; we still get a trophy. Now let's talk about the hockey."

I double-check to make sure everyone's listening. I've been through enough championship games as a coach and player to know that some of these kids are going to self-destruct between now and game time.

"The important thing about championship games is not to think about winning or losing, okay? Whatever you do, do not go home thinking: 'Gee, wouldn't it be great if we win?' or 'I wonder how big the trophies are.' Okay? Don't think about winning or trophies. That's what losers do. What you want to think about is what you do best as a player and what we do best as a team." For a minute I consider asking each one of them what that might be, but I realize many parents are anxious to get going. "So if I were a defenceman, I'd be thinking about taking the puck off of guys, or passing to my forwards, or clearing our zone. If I were a forward, I'd picture myself receiving passes along the boards, passing out front, or shooting the puck past their goalie. Okay? Don't think about winning. Think about what you do best and keep telling yourself 'I'm going to have a great game. I'm going to play my best.' That's what you want to think about. Alright?"

As usual, their reply is a quiet nod. I end it by telling them to get a good night's sleep and to remember we're the team that keeps getting better. The kids and parents head off to their cars. As they do, I suddenly feel it was pointless to have said anything. Everyone's much too excited. Still, it gives me a starting point for my pre-game tomorrow.

On the way to the parking lot, Mike and my wife are chatting away, both clearly excited. By contrast, I feel relaxed, like someone who just picked up the last piece to a puzzle and oddly enough, it fits. Even the team we'll be playing tomorrow seems strangely appropriate. Our opponents are the same ones who have played the biggest part in our season from start to finish. They're now on a two-month undefeated streak. They have talent and coaches used to winning championships. They've pushed and chased us right from the first time we met. Tomorrow afternoon it all comes down to us and the boys in black, the Giants.

 **EVERYTHING THE HARD WAY**

Early Sunday morning I head to the camera shop to load up on film for the game. On the drive over, I'm thinking about what to say in the dressing room this afternoon. What can I say that I haven't said already? Is there anything I've missed?

As I walk in to the store, the Falcons coach walks out.

"Hey, I guess I should thank you," I say, stopping him at the door. "That was quite the win you pulled off last night."

"Oh yeah, I guess it helped you, didn't it? But actually, it's me who should be thanking you. We told the boys beforehand that since we weren't going to the final, we'd make this our championship game. The way you guys were cheering made it feel like the real thing. You should've seen our dressing room after."

"Really? You could hear it down on the ice?"

"Goodness, how could you not? I don't think my players could hear anything else."

It seems odd that he would thank me, but he's genuinely grateful. It sounds like we helped end their season on a high note.

"I can tell you one thing," he continues, "our players will all be at the game this afternoon and we're cheering for you guys. Hopefully, we'll return the favour."

"Thanks."

The game starts at four thirty at the only arena in town in which we haven't played. It's part of a championship weekend the league puts together—one championship game after another, all day long. Immediately following each game, team trophies and individual awards are presented. They ask all teams to attend and players to wear their jerseys. With parents, grandparents, aunts, uncles and friends, it's a raucous crowd and a great playing experience.

We arrive with the whole family just after three o'clock. Under protest, my fourteen-year-old daughter has agreed to take pictures and tape the game on our Camcorder. One disadvantage of being behind the bench is you don't get enough pictures of your kids. This time we will.

Over half the team is already there when I arrive, or at least, they've dropped their equipment in our dressing room and are watching the game before us. It's the Silver division championship for our age group so most of them know someone on the ice. The stands are full and reacting loudly to every play.

Despite the environment, I don't feel nervous at all. Even more surprising, for once I don't feel like I've forgotten anything. I know what I want to say in my pre-game—it isn't written down but I've been thinking about it most of the day—and we'll go with the same lines we've been using for the past month.

"Hey T.J. Is it true the Giants' coaches won it all last year?" asks Justin's dad outside our dressing room.

"Yup. And they won Joe's age group too. Every year they coach two teams and they always do well. In fact, their older boys' team is in the final again this year. I haven't heard who won."

"Seriously?"

"They're good coaches. Their teams always play well."

He raises an eyebrow, as if this has unnerved him. Then he taps my arm and wishes me luck.

A few minutes later, one of the Giants' coaches stops me in the hallway. "Hey, did you hear? We just won the older boys."

"What—again? I guess that means you have to forfeit our game. They put in this new rule—you're only allowed one championship a day."

He laughs. "You know what they say: two's better than one."

It's my turn to laugh. We shake hands and wish each other well. With a half hour to go, it's time to gather the boys in the dressing room.

As I'm rounding them up, Ryan's dad asks about my plans after the game. I don't have any. "If you like," he says, "there's a restaurant down the road that has room for everyone. What do you think?"

"Sounds great. We can either celebrate together or . . . not."

He laughs and promises to have them set aside an area for fifty.

True to form the kids are quiet and almost businesslike in getting their equipment on. The parents however, are nervous—checking and double-checking their son's equipment, trying to make sure everything's perfect. Quite a few sticks get retaped and at least half the boys are asked about their skates: "Too tight? Too loose? You sure?" I keep an eye on the clock. I want five minutes with the boys, but I want it to be the last five minutes—no waiting around after I've finished.

"So we made it," I start, at exactly 4:25 P.M. The boys are all dressed and seated around the room. "The team that gets better just kept getting better and better all the way to the championship. So now, I guess the Giants have a problem. 'Cause as well as we played yesterday, we're going to play even better today."

Turner nods. Tommy pumps his glove in the air.

I quickly review our strategy, but only the basics, and exactly the way we learned them. Defence clear the puck up the boards, where the forwards should be waiting. Follow the play up the ice. Centres are the third defence in our zone and work the breakout with the wingers. Once in the other team's end, we take the puck in wide, draw the defence with us, then pass back to the other winger, in front of their net. We've added some faceoff plays and a couple of different attack plays but before this game, I deliberately keep it simple.

Nerves haven't been an issue with us, but second on my list is something I'm hoping will make sure anyone feeling anxious, looks at it a different way. "You know how good we are at quick starts. Well today, it's more important than ever. You know why?" A few shrug. "Because the Giants are going to be nervous. Right? Think about it—a championship game. Playing the number one team. I'll bet some of those guys are really nervous. So let's see if we can't score a few goals right at the start when they may not be playing so well."

The last thing I want to do is a quick run around the room, making sure each player has no doubt what they do best for the team. I start by reminding them we want to play our best in the championship, and then let each player know what I think they're best at. I keep it short—just a phrase or two each. "Travis—shot; one a shift, okay? Ryan—speed and pass; no one catches you today, right? Simon—covering the guy out front. Mike—speed and deke; no goalie stops your deke. Braeden—taking the puck, shooting it up the boards; you're best in the league." And so on. Almost on cue, as I finish with the last player, Dennis comes in and tells us they're ready to start the player introductions—goalie first, then players, numbers two through sixteen. Last out will be the coaches.

The crowd cheers as each player skates onto the ice. We line up along the blue line as if awaiting the national anthem. But once the introductions are finished, the referee signals for the warm-up to begin. Seeing the referee, I'm disappointed. I recognize her from Joe's league. She's horribly inconsistent—flagrant penalties get missed, then a marginal one is called. There are worse referees but she's definitely below average.

I scan the Giants as they skate in their end. They're a solid team with a few standouts. Number four is a big, strong, fast centre. He finished Top Ten in scoring and beat us single handedly the first time we faced them. Numbers twelve and sixteen are both speedy forwards who ended up Top Twenty. Their goalie is big and covers the angles well. Of the kids who played more than five games in net, he had the best goals against average. No doubt—the Giants deserve to be here.

The ref arrives at our bench. "We need a game puck," she says.

"Here you go," replies George. He retrieves a baggie from his pocket, filled with ice. He opens it and pulls out a puck. It's an official Toronto Maple Leaf puck.

"Wow, frozen and everything," I say.

"Hey, it's the championship game. Got to have a decent puck."

The ref smiles and takes it to centre ice.

As the warm-up ends, I call Mike, Ryan and Will to the bench. "Okay guys, you're up first. Don't forget, quick start now." All three nod and head to centre.

The ref raises her hand and the crowd quiets. The players get into position. Andrew and Connor skate to our blue line. The ref checks the goalies. They nod. The puck hits the ice.

True to form, we're off quickly. Twenty seconds in, Mike knocks the puck behind the Giants' defence and he's in the clear. With a Giant in hot pursuit he nudges it further ahead—a flat out breakaway.

"We're on our way boys," I yell at the bench.

Not this time. On the freshly flooded ice, the puck slides too fast for Mike to catch it in time. It hits the end boards, but he's on it and centres. The Giants' defence intercept, but their clearing shot goes straight to Andrew. He passes to Ryan who just misses on the short side. It's early, but we're all over them.

Next out are Travis, Joel and Kevin. "Remember Travis, a shot every shift, okay? Joel, Kevin, use your speed."

For the past couple of months Robert has been a calm, cool presence on our defence. Time after time, when the pressure is on, he beats an opponent to the puck, or takes it away, and calmly makes a great pass to start our attack. I've paired him with Patrick who has a tendency to wander. Early in the second shift, the Giants get the puck in our zone but Robert does it again, calmly passing off to Joel at the hash marks. There's a bit of a scrum at our blue line but Kevin gets control and knocks it toward centre ice. Travis beats everyone to the puck, swerves right, then left. He's in the clear and lets his shot go from inside the faceoff circle. It's a rocket, high into the mesh on the glove side. The crowd roars. We're up one-nothing.

Justin's line is out next for their first shift. Once again, we're pressing in their zone. Turner centres but it's intercepted. The Giants are really crowding the front of the net. It reminds me of our Christmas tournament when we constantly had all five linemates in front of our goal.

"Look at them," I say to the kids on the bench. "See how they're all in front of their net. You guys know what that means, right? They won't be able to clear it. Defence—play your position on the blue line and watch for their clearing passes. As soon as you get it, send it right back in on them. You know what I mean?"

Braeden and Simon nod. We went over it so many times at the tournament, they probably do remember. But just to be sure, I explain again how five teammates in front of their own net means there's no one to pass to. When they shoot it out, we can be first to the puck.

It seems to work. Halfway through the period, the Giants still don't have a shot. But the play is becoming choppy and the Giants are getting desperate. Following a scrum in their end, they fire it down the ice. Our defence intercept, but the Giants are quickly on the puck. They shoot it deep into our zone and give chase. From the corner, a Giant takes an impossible shot. Tommy covers as the puck sails across the top of the crease to the opposite corner. Another Giant shoots it straight back across the crease again. The first Giant stops the puck and tries to carry it into the net. He falls in the crease. Robert and the Giants' number four both try to dig the puck out from underneath him, while Tommy tries to get back in the play. But Tommy's blocked out perfectly and number four pushes the puck into the net. Tie game.

"What about the goalie interference?" shouts Brad toward the ref.

She doesn't even glance our way and calmly skates to centre ice. I promised myself I wouldn't say anything to the ref today, so instead I turn to the boys. "Come on guys, we'll get it back. We're playing well."

Justin's line is next with Braeden and Simon on defence. After the Giants shoot it in to our end, Braeden starts a perfect breakout that sends Turner screaming into their zone. He shoots from the hash marks, but just misses. They try to clear but Justin intercepts. He dekes by one Giant then another. He's momentarily in the clear but the second Giant swings his back leg around to trip Justin beautifully. Justin goes down and the puck slides harmlessly through the slot. Once again there's no call. It probably was accidental but it was also leg on leg and cost us a goal. I can't believe Justin wouldn't have scored with that much time and room.

The pattern continues for the rest of the period. The Giants crowd the front of their net making it difficult for our guys to get through. "Use the pass, okay forwards, just like in practice." I remind them of the drill we've done in almost every full-ice practice for the past two months. A forward carries the puck to one side, supported by the other. As soon as their defencemen come to that side, we pass it to the third forward, in front of the net. Will, Mike and Ryan run it to perfection to get two shots from point blank range. Neither goes in. Kevin sets up Joel but number four takes him down from behind before he can shoot. The buzzer sounds.

"Okay, we're playing great," I say to the boys on the bench. "We're skating, we're getting shots. If we keep on like this, we'll be fine."

The second period starts with us pushing into the Giants' zone. They're still crowding the middle of the ice and chasing the puck relentlessly. One of their clearing shots heads toward Robert. It looks harmless enough but number four is bearing down on him. The puck slides under the heel of Robert's stick, and suddenly the Giants have a break. Robert turns and gives chase but number four is too fast. He closes in on Tommy from the left-hand side. He waits, waits, then at the last second shoots high. It looks like he left it too late but as he circles the net he raises his hands in the air. The ref arrives after the play and signals goal.

As I watch her pick up the puck from in front of the net, I'm replaying the shot in my mind. I'm sure there was no room to score. "How did that go in?" I ask Brad. "I heard two clangs—one off the crossbar, one off the post. It ended up in the crease. So how did it go in?"

"It's pretty hard to tell from here," he replies.

"Yeah but physically, how could it happen? It can't hit the crossbar, the post, and still go in. It's impossible."

Brad shrugs. The net is at the far end of the rink so there's no way to claim I had a better view. But the ref was a good twenty feet away when the puck allegedly entered the net. So she didn't see either.

"Hey, Coach," says Braeden excitedly, arriving at the bench, "the puck never went in. It hit the crossbar. It didn't cross the line."

"Are you sure?" I ask.

"Yeah. I was right there. I saw it."

Braeden arrived at the net just as the Giants' player shot. I remember seeing him. He's always been one of those kids who tells it exactly the way it is. I signal to the referee and she skates over. "Ref, my players are saying that wasn't a goal. Are you absolutely sure the puck crossed the line?"

"Yup. It was in," she replies, smiling.

There isn't a shred of doubt in her voice. I'm positive she didn't see it. Still, as she answers, it occurs to me how pointless it was to ask. What did I expect her to say: "No sir, it wasn't a goal. That's why I've brought everyone to centre ice"? Once again I've let myself get distracted. She signalled goal. It's over. Time to focus on getting it back.

"Justin," I call as he leaves the bench. "Don't forget that play we've been practising, okay? Draw their defence to one side, then pass it to Turner. And Turner—we need lots of forechecking, okay? Luke—we're playing Raptors, right?" The boys nod and quickly get into position.

As soon as the puck drops we're all over them. In seconds the puck is in the Giants' zone with Cougars chasing it everywhere. Both sides are desperate, making the play scrambly, particularly when the puck gets close to their net. Suddenly, Justin picks up the puck in the corner and fires from an impossible angle. Their goalie isn't covering the post. As the puck deflects in off his skate the crowd roars once again. Tie game: two-two.

Mike's line is out next and keeps up the pressure. The play is all in the Giants' end. When one of their defence coughs up the puck, Mike takes it and wheels around two more defenders. He fires. The goalie saves it but the rebound heads straight for Ryan. In front of the open net, the puck skips over his stick. The Giants clear and break into our zone. Mike stickchecks the puck away and gives chase, but a Giant slides into him skates first, taking his legs out. Instantly the linesman's hand is in the air.

"Tripping," shouts one of our players.

"It's okay, they got it," I reply.

Will picks up the puck and banks it off the boards to Ryan. Suddenly he's in the clear. Mike's up and skating hard. He's caught up to Ryan—it's two on none. Ryan carries it down one side and shoots, aiming for the top corner. It nicks the crossbar and sails into the netting above the glass. The ref blows her whistle.

Meanwhile, the boy who slid into Mike has been slow getting to his feet. The linesman helps him to the Giants' bench, and then skates for the faceoff circle. As he passes our bench, I stop him.

"What about the penalty?"

"There was no penalty," he replies.

"You had your hand in the air."

The linesman shakes his head as if to say, No I didn't.

George quickly intervenes. "Before that player got injured," he says, pointing to the Giant now on the bench, "he tripped our player and you put your hand in the air. I clearly saw you raise your hand. You were standing by the boards at the blue line."

The linesman crinkles his brow. It's obvious he's forgotten. Still, George is so sure, the linesman goes to the ref for a conference, then returns. "Neither one of us had our hand in the air," he says. "I don't know what you saw but there's no penalty."

"Brutal," replies George, shaking his head.

The delay seems to affect the game. For the balance of the period, the play is choppy with neither side able to sustain an attack. The puck is mainly in the neutral zone and their end. As the buzzer sounds to signal just twelve minutes to go, I'm worried Tommy hasn't had enough shots to keep him sharp. He stops by the bench for some water as we change ends for the final time.

"Tommy, how're you doing?" I ask as his dad squirts water into his mouth.

"Good," he replies, calmly.

Brad gives him last minute pointers on covering the post and being quick in the crease. Tommy listens attentively, nodding to show he understands and he's ready.

The third period starts and once again, play is choppy. A Giants' forward enters our zone and reaches for the puck. Travis, catching him from behind, lifts his stick. The kid loses his balance and goes down. Travis picks up the puck and the ref blows her whistle. It's a penalty.

"What was that?" asks Brad. "He didn't touch him."

It is an odd play to call as a penalty but, unfortunately, it's the kind of call she's become notorious for in Joe's league. With the score tied in the third period of a championship game, we'll have to play shorthanded.

Although the puck stays in our end for the entire two minutes, there's only a few good scoring chances and Tommy's equal to the task. The rest of the time, our boys do a great job of keeping the puck outside, along the boards. Although we miss a couple of chances to clear, and it's definitely tense, the score remains two-two when the Giants' manpower advantage ends. Joel, Kevin, Robert and Patrick had to kill the entire penalty by themselves but they did it.

When Justin, Turner and Luke take to the ice, they're well rested and ready. Like earlier shifts they're forechecking hard. On the rare occasion when the Giants do manage to shoot the puck by them, Braeden's reading the play, getting to the puck and firing it right back in again. After almost a minute of constant pressure, their hard work finally pays off. Turner centres the puck, a Giant intercepts but can only shoot it behind the net. It bounces off the boards to Justin who once again banks it in off the side of the goalie. The crowd roars. We're up three-two.

Mike's line takes to centre ice. They've won all their shifts and had numerous chances, but today, they seem snake-bitten around the net. Once again, a neat three-way passing play ends on Ryan's stick in the slot. But whereas he shot high earlier, this time he can't raise it high enough and it bounces off the goalie's pads. It's a shot he's buried numerous times throughout the season.

On the very next shift, the Giants get a bit of a breakthrough. They fire the puck into our end and after some forechecking of their own, number four gets not one but two good wraparound chances. Fortunately, Tommy and Connor read them well to stop both. When play resumes we clear it out of our end and once again, put the pressure on.

With three minutes left, even though it's only a one-goal game, it looks like we're going to do it. The Giants are playing determined hockey and are making it difficult for us to score, but they're not generating enough chances of their own. They work together to stop us but they're not working together to score. From start to finish the pattern's been the same. The Giants react to our playmaking, do their best to stop us, then fire the puck away. Their scoring chances come off bounces and clearing shots.

"Defence," I say on the bench, "let's make sure we play our position okay? Don't let anyone get behind you. We've got the lead. There's only a few minutes left."

With a minute to go, they pull their goalie. He steps onto their bench, just as we fire it back into their end. Joel, Travis and Kevin are pressing. It looks like we might score. They get the puck a couple of times but the Giants are even more desperate. The puck isn't staying on anyone's stick for long.

Travis backhands toward the corner but one of the Giants intercepts and tries to clear. Braeden beats everyone to the puck and shoots it back into their zone. But two Giants crash into him as he does. With Braeden down just outside their blue line, a Giant fires the puck high off the boards, the length of the ice. Good, I think to myself, icing. That'll finish it. I watch the puck cross the goal line and wait for the whistle. There's none. I look for the ref, then the linesman. Neither have their hand in the air. Instead, they're watching the play.

"Call the icing!" shouts Brad.

A Giants forechecker is first to the puck and centres. Two more Giants are all alone in front of our net. Tommy makes the first save but the rebound slides under his outstretched arm. The crowd roars. There's eight seconds showing on the clock. We're tied again, three-three. I can't believe it.

"The only reason they have an icing rule is exactly that play," fumes Brad. "When another team is pressing you, you're not supposed to just fire it down the ice to a cherry picker. How could they not see that?"

Suddenly my heart is pounding. I'm no longer relaxed. I don't even consider protesting. I know there's nothing I can do. But as the players in black celebrate, it's much more than this play I'm upset about. Everything that's happened today makes sense to me now. The missed chances, the missed calls. This isn't our day and we're going to lose.

"Okay boys, focus," I say to Justin, Turner and Luke as they take to the ice. "Remember that drill we do—ten seconds to score. We've only got eight but let's see if we can do it."

The three of them nod and head for the faceoff circle. The Giants' number four stays out and wins the faceoff. The puck comes to Luke but number four knocks it off his stick and carries the puck into our zone on the right side, skating hard to get by our defence. I quickly glance at the clock. It's still on eight seconds.

"Start the clock!" I yell.

It's too late. Number four is behind our defence. He leans down on his stick and fires, high, stick side. The puck just misses and lands in the corner. After a brief flurry in the faceoff circle, the buzzer finally sounds. We're headed for overtime.

"Come on guys," I say, gathering everyone at the bench. "We can do this. All game long we've been the better team. They're lucky we haven't scored ten goals. And what's worse for them, we're the team that gets better. So if they thought we were tough in regulation time, wait'll they see us in overtime. Okay? Let's go."

I don't believe a word I'm saying. I've been in too many playoff and championship games. This isn't the way it goes for the winners. On the days you win, everything goes your way—the bounces, the calls, everything. Whenever the other team has a chance, they can't seem to close the deal. Exactly what's happening to us. We've had breakaways, guys in the clear, rebounds in the crease, three-way passing plays, all go awry. Two of the Giants' goals came on missed calls; the other didn't even go in. To me, it's obvious—this is their day and they're going to win.

Overtime is ten minutes of sudden death. First to score, wins. If we're still tied, we'll play another overtime. The puck drops but my mind is only half on the game. The other half bemoans how unfair it is that we have to lose.

The pattern of the game continues. Shift after shift, we look for our teammates, trying to manufacture scoring plays. The Giants are desperate, crowding the net and playing courageously. Justin's line speeds into the Giants' end and keeps the play there for most of a minute, but no shots get through. Mike's line takes over, keeps the play in their end, but no shots reach the goalie. Travis' line comes on and executes a slick three-way passing play ending with Joel's shot, but it's tipped at the last minute. Then Travis finds an opening and lets a better wrist shot go than the one he scored on. Their goalie makes his best save of the game. After one overtime period nothing is settled.

The second overtime produces more of the same. Justin's line is once again all over the Giants. Turner shoots along the ice only to be stopped by a last second pad save. Then, in a goalmouth scramble, Justin finds the puck and shoots. Their goalie thinks it's in and looks behind him. The ref blows her whistle and races in. The goalie stands up. The puck is on the goal line. Game on.

The acoustics are such that I haven't been able to hear what the Giants' coaches are saying. But the desperation hockey in their zone continues. Will, Travis, Ryan all get shots that can't find their way through the maze of players in front of the net. Number four gets a chance of his own but Mike and Connor converge on him at the same time, creating a Giants sandwich inside our blue line. Mike skates away with the puck but then is checked to the ice himself. For the balance of the second overtime, play is mostly in the neutral zone and scoring chances are nullified before the puck reaches the net.

As the buzzer sounds the VP House League calls the coaches together.

"Guys, it's been a great game but we have to settle this," he says. "We're already a half hour behind and there's two games to go."

It suddenly occurs to me the crowd has grown. None of our fans have left, and the parents and players for the next game are starting to arrive. No doubt there's also people from the rink adjacent who've heard a championship game has gone into double overtime.

"Here's what we'll do," the VP continues. "There'll be a two-minute period of four-on-four, followed by three-on-three, then two-on-two, then one-on-one."

"Sudden death?" asks a Giants' coach.

"That's right. First goal wins. And guys, I want you to use your whole bench, not just the good players, okay?"

We all nod.

Justin's line is due out so we send Justin, Turner, Braeden and Simon out for the four-on-four. The play continues as a carbon copy of the game. Over the entire two minutes there's shots but no real scoring chances. The kids are too desperate. The buzzer sounds.

For the three-on-three, it's Mike's turn, with Luke, and Robert on defence. I know the Giants will choose number four and I've already decided I'll leave Mike out as long as number four's there. Mike doesn't have his usual wind today but he's our top player and number four is theirs. Might as well let the two decide it.

It's not to be. For some reason, the Giants' coaches keep number four on the bench. He finished the game so it's not his turn, but I still expected to see him, especially with Mike out. Could this be our break?

The puck drops and Mike pokes it ahead. The Giants' centre turns and fires it into our end. Robert retrieves and flips it up the boards. A Giants' player intercepts. Mike's on him quickly and steals the puck. He nudges it into the open ice and races toward their end. The last Giants' defender has the angle but Mike's digging hard. By their blue line, he's a stride ahead. The Giant slashes at his stick and legs but Mike fends him off. He cuts to the goal and shoots.

He scores!

For the shot that ends the season, Mike chooses the one he's always said gives the goalies the most trouble—on the ice, inside the corner. He wheels around and races to our end, pumping his stick wildly. Our bench empties and the crowd goes bananas.

"Yeah!" I scream, pumping my own fist. The relief is tremendous. George, Brad and I shake hands, and then head out onto the ice. In seconds there's a junk pile of Cougars at centre. Shedding their sticks and gloves on the way, they all open their arms and dive into one another. Joel has taken off his helmet and after diving in once, gets up from the pile, looks around with that huge smile of his, and not knowing what to do, simply turns and dives back in again.

As I leave the bench I notice my heart's not pounding any more. I'm thinking of the boys and how this could be a memory they hang onto. I want to make sure I get to every kid and tell him how unbelievably great he played. Mike's one of the last but

I grab him under the armpits and lift him high in the air. "You did it!" I say. "Can you believe that?"

A wry little grin forms under his helmet.

I put him down and give him a tight hug, whispering in his ear: "Way to go bud. I'm proud of you."

The league officials quickly start the presentations. "Ladies and Gentlemen," announces Dennis from the players' side of the rink, "let's put our hands together for an entertaining, well-fought game." The fans roar in agreement. "This year's finalists are the Giants," he continues, introducing each player beginning with the goalie. The players come forward to receive their trophy and a handshake from the VP House League. When he announces the Giants' coaches, the VP spreads his hands wide as if to say, what happened—don't you guys always win?

"For this year's Minor Novice Gold division champions," continues Dennis, "I call on Mike O'Grady to accept the trophy."

A few minutes earlier, they'd asked me to pick a captain, something I don't believe in for kids' teams. I gave them Mike's name but while they were handing out the Giants' trophies, I told Mike I'd be sending the whole team over with him, and to make sure the trophy got passed around. So when Dennis calls on Mike, the entire group of Cougars follows.

The trophy is the same one used for all championship games, but I'm sure the kids think it's theirs alone, to be kept in somebody's house for the next year. It's two feet high and mostly wood, capped off with a golden hockey player. Mike receives it, but instantly turns and takes it into the mob of teammates. They circle the ice as a group, holding the trophy high in the air as it passes from one set of small hands to another. Flashbulbs flicker from all corners. Some of the parents are on the benches, hoping for a better view. A few take to the ice themselves.

"This year's Cougars finished in first place for the regular season," continues Dennis once the victory lap is complete, "and are playoff champions. I call on number one, Tommy . . ."

Dennis introduces the team, player by player. Each boy comes forward, receives his two trophies and shakes the VP's hand, pausing for a picture. When they announce the coaches' names, the three of us go up. They only allow two trophies for the coaching staff but we can purchase more at two dollars apiece. We quickly decide the team can afford the eight dollars to ensure all four coaches have the same mementos.

The last order of business is the league's individual awards. After top goalie, Mike's name is called out again as top scorer. As he arrives back, a number of players, and me, want to get a look at the plaque.

Once all the awards have been handed out, a photographer from the local paper tells me he wants a picture. The team gets together with its trophies for one last on ice photo, and then it's off to the dressing room.

Will's mom has arranged for *We Are The Champions* to be playing as we enter the room. All the parents are waiting; the room is wall-to-wall people. Everyone's laughing, smiling, patting each other on the back—it's a great scene. As Mike sits on the bench next to me, pulling off his sweater, George emerges from the throng.

"Here you go bud, you earned it." He hands Mike the game puck.

Mike looks at me with bewildered eyes. "What's that for?"

"The championship puck," answers George. "You got the winner so I picked you as MVP. I know it probably won't fit in your trophy case with all those other awards."

Mike laughs and thanks him, as do I. It's a nice touch on a day when many players stood out—Justin, Travis, Joel, Turner, Ryan, Will, not to mention Robert and Braeden. I can't think of a single player who had an off game. Kevin and Luke had shots that could've been the winner. Andrew, Simon and Connor were in position all game and Patrick made several good clearing passes. There was more flow to our game last night against the Wildcats, but thinking it through, everyone on our team came to play. Tommy might've had the toughest job of all—staying focused during long stretches without a shot—but he too played tough, particularly in overtime, when he stopped number four a few times. Then again, with a different ref, he might've had a shutout.

After half an hour, the dressing room is all but empty. Most have left for the restaurant and Will's parents are begging him to hurry up. The team trophy remains in the room. Brad and I are there but our sons have left to watch the next game.

"Hey, could I get a picture with you guys and the big trophy?" asks Will's dad.

Will grabs the trophy while Brad and I take a knee with our arms on his shoulder. For the past month or so, Will has developed a habit of playing most of the game with only one hand on his stick. Time and time again we've reminded him to use two hands. Now, he needs no such reminder.

"Hey Will," says Brad, pointing to the trophy, "two hands!"

Sure enough, the boy with the fondness for one hand on the stick has two hands on the trophy. No doubt his father got a picture with two coaches and an eight-year-old sharing a pretty big laugh.

At the restaurant, the boys have all gathered at one table while the parents occupy another. But unlike our earlier experiences, the room is quiet. I make a point of visiting as many parents as I can to tell them how well their son played and how much I enjoyed coaching them, both of which are true. But as I walk around the room, I find myself drawn to the kids. They're different tonight. They chat with one another but there's a calmness to them I haven't seen before. Each one of them has this amazing grin on his face, one that for tonight at least, won't go away. They're glowing. I doubt that anyone in the restaurant would ever guess these boys are hockey players. But they are. And for tonight, they're champions.

ODDS AND ENDS

Kevin's mom arranged a team party to officially end the season. It was a great time with lots of speeches, jokes, memories recounted and plenty of good food. But a year later, my most enduring memory is still the kids in the restaurant that night we won. The looks on their faces, how calm, and happy they were. The games, practices, good and bad plays come back when I think long enough, or when someone else reminds me, but the memory that pops to mind when someone says Cougar is those kids at the table—the glowing eyes and those amazing grins.

As for how much of the story is fact and how much is remembered through a coach's rose-coloured glasses, most of our season was written down. All goals, assists and penalties were recorded on game sheets (signed by the referee); the regular season and playoff stats were tabulated on an Internet site, and there were over six hundred e-mails that passed through my computer relating to the team. I have ensured everything written herein agrees with all of those pieces of paper. Further, the championship game was recorded on a DVD as well as video by my daughter on our Camcorder. My description of the game agrees fully with those recordings (i.e. the Giants' second goal did not go in, their third was scored off a clear icing, and the linesman did put his hand in the air when Mike was tripped—though in fairness, it appears he was signalling a delayed offside).

With respect to names, I've changed everyone's in order to protect the privacy of the people on our team, as well as anyone involved peripherally with the story. The exceptions are Mike, Joe, Sarah and Walter Gretzky. I don't believe this is a story about specific individuals. The situations we encountered are common to most towns, regions and even other sports.

In terms of where they are now, Travis, Ryan, Joel, Justin and Turner have gone on to play Rep hockey, all on teams that met with mixed success. Most of the others have continued playing in our town's Gold House League. Tommy, Robert and Kevin were on the team that won the playoff championship the next season, coached by Kevin's dad and Brad. Luke's team finished first, but lost in the final. Andrew got his wish to play goalie for a team in the Silver League—the Giants, no less. George claims to have retired from coaching but still has the same sense of humour, forever telling it how it is in a way that makes everyone, or at least me, laugh.

As for Mike, after much debate, we decided we didn't want him playing Rep. But two weeks before the tryouts, he pulled us aside and asked if he could, promising it would only be for a year. Rep hockey gets bashed a fair bit around our house, but friends of his said the team really wanted him. We said yes and he made the same team that cut him the year before. Although they wouldn't release player stats, they told us after the season that he finished top three in team scoring. It was a fast group of boys but they never came together and finished middle of the pack. I applied to coach them the following season but was turned down.

I did coach Joe's team. We finished a point out of first and won the Playoff Championship. Guess who my assistants were? That's right—the Giants' coaches. We had a lot of laughs and all of us, including our kids, have become good friends.

I wrote the book because I felt our season encapsulated all that's good and bad about kids' sports. Unfortunately, it's impossible for me to sign off without putting in black and white what readers have no doubt concluded for themselves: most of the good comes from the kids and most of the bad comes from the adults. Good intentions are everywhere but fairness, consistency and integrity are not. We can do better.

In any event, if you've never tried hockey, you should. And keep your stick on the ice. You just never know what will happen.

To order additional copies of *Coaching Kids' Hockey: the Good, the Bad and the Unbelievable*, just fill out the order form below and mail it to:

**Kookaburra Press,
1011 Upper Middle Road East, Suite 1406,
Oakville, Ontario L6H 5Z9**

Alternatively, log onto **www.coachingkidshockey.com**
and place your order via our website.

BOOK ORDER COUPON

Please send me _____ copies of *Coaching Kids' Hockey: The Good, The Bad and The Unbelievable* @**$21.95** each

Shipping and handling will be added to each order. $2 for first book, $1 for each additional book. Not applicable on orders of more than five books.

Canadian residents add 7% GST

TOTAL AMOUNT ENCLOSED $ _____
Payment Method (check one)
  ❏ Cheque
  ❏ Money Order
  ❏ Visa
  ❏ Mastercard

Card # _____

Expiry _____

Signature _____

Name_____

Address_____

City_____ Province _____

Postal Code_____ Phone _____

Please make all cheques payable to **Kookaburra Press**